SANDEEP MARWAH

A GLOBAL LAUREATE OF ART & CULTURE

Sushil Bharti

rahi publication
A Publishing House
NEW DELHI

Published by Rahi Publication 2026

First edition published in English
by Rahi Publications in 2026

Rahi Publication

rahipublications@gmail.com
www.rahipublication.in

ISBN 978-93-91532-43-7

Printed and Bounded in India

CONTENTS

Beyond the Sands of Time

Many books have been written before this one in an attempt to understand the life of Sandeep Marwah ji — books that speak of his family's journey. But reading through all of them, I found that they speak more about his work, or about things that Sandeep Marwah ji himself has said at some point — either from a stage or in conversation with the author. It has always seemed to me that when a person tells their own story, they tend to present it in a way that suits them — shaping and polishing it a little — which makes it somewhat difficult for the reader to understand them as they truly are.

In this book, I have written about Sandeep Marwah ji's family background and his early life and struggles, while also attempting to understand what his personality is genuinely like. This could not have been achieved simply by reading about him — it also required understanding his thoughts and actions at the level of lived reality. Perhaps this is where my writing may differ from that of other authors, because I have known him for nearly fifteen years. I have been a participant in many of his endeavours. I am familiar with his thinking. I have been a witness to the consistency — or otherwise — between what he says and what he does.

For a writer, it is essential to write what they wish to write — not what they are made to write. I believe that I too am a witness to one part of Sandeep Marwah ji's journey. Through everything I experienced while being in his company during that journey, and then when I held it against what I knew of his thinking, I found that in his actions he is a genuinely sincere karmayogi — a person devoted to righteous work.

I had wanted to write this book much earlier, but as is my habit of sometimes deferring today's work to tomorrow, I paid a price for it. What happened was this: I had written several chapters, but between the excuse of time, the policy of "we'll do it later," and the occasional "I'm not in the mood right now", one day I discovered that everything I had written had been lost in a hard drive crash. It was a great setback, and despite every effort, the lost material could not be recovered. They say that what is meant to happen, happens. Because of this, and because more time became available to me, I had the opportunity to understand Sandeep ji further — and my sense of his personality has now become even more firmly established.

Perhaps it was for the best. What I had written earlier may not have been able to give the reader the depth that I believe this writing will provide. I hope this book will not only help you understand Sandeep ji's personality, but will also inspire you to reflect on what a person's life ought to be. The rest is for you to decide — how you receive it. I have said everything I had to say.

— Sushil Bharti
Writer and Filmmaker

SANDEEP MARWAH

A GLOBAL LAUREATE OF ART & CULTURE

1

A Priceless Legacy Forged from Ashes

Whenever a writer is deeply moved by a personality and decides to write about their life, they do not merely record events — they attempt to reach the very roots of that person. To truly understand any human being, it is not enough to look at who they are today; it is equally essential to know the background hidden behind them, their family's history, the circumstances of their era, and the story of the values instilled in them. This is precisely why, when the thought of writing about Sandeep Marwah's life first came to me, I realized that to understand the depth of his personality, I would need to know his family and his past.

Sandeep Marwah is a personality defined not only by his achievements, but also by his values, his sensitivity, and his human qualities. In him, one can see all the virtues that every parent dreams of seeing in their child — hard work, discipline, compassion, self-confidence, and the desire to do something meaningful for society. But such qualities do not emerge by chance; behind them lie generations of struggle, lived experience, and the difficult chapters of life.

To speak honestly, the idea of writing a book on Sandeep Marwah had come to me quite early. Yet I did not rush. When you write about someone's life, it is not merely a task of words — it is a task of responsibility. So I took my time. I listened to him, understood him, and tried to learn about his background. Every chapter I have written in this book is either something I personally witnessed during the time I spent with him, or something I heard directly from him — and this is the very reason I was able to understand his personality at such a profound level.

I have listened to him speak on many platforms. Whenever he shares a part of his life's story, he often speaks of his father. He tells how, at the time of the India-Pakistan Partition, his father came to Delhi from Pakistan at just eighteen years of age. Each time I heard this story, a new question was born in my mind — what other chapters might lie behind that story? Where were that family's roots? And through what circumstances had they arrived here?

This curiosity urged me to dig a little deeper. The information that gradually came to light made one thing clear: this was not merely the story of one man, but the story of an entire era's struggle.

The family of Sandeep Marwah's great-grandfather Mohanlal ji and grandfather Sewaram ji was known, in its time, as a distinguished and prosperous family in the city of Peshawar. In Peshawar's Raja Bazaar, they ran a large departmental store in their name. It was no ordinary shop — it stocked nearly everything related to bakery goods, and also housed a wine shop. Given the social and economic environment of those times, obtaining a liquor license was no small matter. It was considered, in itself, a mark of prestige and trust.

The store also supplied the British Army on a regular basis. This meant their trade was not confined to the local level — it was connected to the administrative and military establishment of the time. In that era, this family was counted among the prosperous and respected families of Peshawar. There was no want in the household, and life moved along in an orderly manner.

But no one knows when the wheel of history will turn, or in which direction.

Sandeep Marwah's father, Suraj Prakash Marwah, was the youngest among his brothers. He had two elder brothers — the eldest was Shri Krishan Lal Marwah, and the second was Shyam Marwah. Life was moving at its usual pace when, without warning, the terrible year of 1947 arrived — and with it, a moment that would change the face of the entire subcontinent.

The Partition of India and Pakistan was not merely a political event; it became the most painful chapter in the lives of millions. People who had lived alongside one another for generations — who shared bonds of kinship, friendship, and neighbourly warmth — suddenly found a wall of mistrust and fear rising between them.

Riots broke out. Fire, violence, and chaos descended with such ferocity that every person was consumed by the struggle to save their own life. Neighbours who had been one's own only yesterday seemed suddenly to turn into enemies. Everywhere, the same cry was heard: Hindus living in Pakistan should go to India, and Muslims living in India should go to Pakistan.

The land was one — but it had now been split in two.

In the midst of this upheaval, an incident occurred that

shook the Marwah family to its very core. During the riots, Suraj Prakash Marwah's elder brother, Shyam Marwah, was shot by rioters. This event made one thing unmistakably clear to the family: it was no longer safe to remain there.

A decision had to be made — they would have to leave behind their land, their roots, and everything they had, and go to Hindustan.

But as difficult as it was to take that decision, it was far more difficult to carry it out. There was simply no time to sell the property that generations had built with such toil. Conditions had deteriorated to the point where each passing day felt as though the next moment could be one's last.

In the end, compelled by circumstances, Suraj Prakash Marwah had to sell that vast departmental store at a throw-away price. A property worth crores changed hands for a mere eighteen thousand rupees. This was not only a financial loss — it was as though the labour and identity of generations were being left behind forever.

The next destination was Delhi.

At that time, the means available to travel from Pakistan to India were desperately few and unsafe. Small aircraft called Dakotas were being used to carry people to Delhi. These planes were ordinarily built for forty passengers, but in those circumstances, sixty or seventy people were somehow crammed into each one.

Whenever a Dakota landed, a stampede would break out at the airport. Everyone rushed towards the plane, for it was the only hope they had of reaching a safe life.

Suraj Prakash Marwah, too, waited at the airport with that same hope. As soon as the plane arrived, he ran with the crowd towards it and somehow managed to board. When the aircraft took off, a momentary wave of relief washed over him.

But then, in an instant, a thought struck him — where was his coat?

He was gripped by panic. He remembered: the coat had been left behind at the airport. If it had only been the coat, perhaps the grief would have been bearable. But tucked inside the inner pocket of that coat were the eighteen thousand rupees — every rupee he had received from selling his entire worldly estate.

That sum was not merely money. It was the last remnant of everything he had ever been.

The ground seemed to shift beneath Suraj Prakash Marwah's feet. But there was nothing to be done now. The plane had already taken off, and the coat hung behind on a hook at the airport.

What had happened was this — the plane had been delayed, and while waiting, he had hung his coat on a peg and lain down to rest. How was he to know that when the plane finally arrived, such a frantic rush would ensue that he would forget to pick up the coat entirely?

All that remained to him now was two hundred rupees in the pocket of his shirt. With a heavy heart and an uncertain future, he arrived in Delhi.

The scenes he encountered upon reaching India were enough to shake any sensitive soul to its depths. Millions of Hindu refugees who had fled Pakistan were living in tents. People who had left behind good homes and land now wandered, adrift, in a strange country.

Suraj Prakash Marwah too became a part of that vast tide of refugees.

For a time, he lived in tents. Later, he found shelter at

Delhi's Purana Qila, the Old Fort, where temporary arrangements had been made for refugees at the time. Life was hard, but gradually, as time passed, the wounds began to heal.

It is said that if a person has learnt to work hard, and has been given strong values by their family, then darkness cannot reign in their life forever.

Slowly, through hard work and patience, Suraj Prakash Marwah began to rebuild his life. He acquired a government house on instalment payments, near Nizamuddin East railway station, the house that would become the witness to his story of struggle and reconstruction.

To put his life back on track, he started with small and modest endeavours. He first worked at the Jodhpur Mess. Later, he was allotted a shop in Khan Market, which in time became known as the Music Shop. This was the place where his diligence and honesty slowly began to give the family a firm foundation.

With the passage of time, hard work began to bear fruit. When a man's intentions are honest and he trusts in his own labour, life gradually finds its way back to the right path. And so it was with Suraj Prakash Marwah. Moving forward, he eventually took a house in the upscale neighbourhood of Defence Colony, and later established his residence in the prestigious locality of Greater Kailash. This was not merely a story of financial success — it was the story of a man who, having lost everything, refused to give up.

If we turn the pages of this story a little further back, we find that Sandeep Marwah's mother, who was born Sheela Khanna, and became Sheela Marwah after her marriage to Suraj Prakash Marwah, and her family too had not been spared by the tragedy of Partition. Her family came first to

Ambala. Sheela ji's elder sister, Nirmal Khanna, had already been married into a distinguished zamindar family in Ambala, her husband's name was M. L. Khanna. It was he who advised his father-in-law, Radhakrishna ji, Sheela ji's father, to come to Ambala in the wake of the Hindu-Muslim riots. And so Sandeep ji's maternal family arrived in Ambala.

The story of Sandeep Marwah's father-in-law, Surendra Kapoor ji, is similarly marked by Partition. His father, Lalchand Kapoor ji, also arrived in Meerut during the division of India. In the early days, struggling to find steady work, Lalchand ji began trading in jaggery. Lalchand Kapoor and the celebrated actor Prithviraj Kapoor were cousins. It was Prithviraj Kapoor who called Surendra Kapoor ji to Mumbai, where he went on to work for eight years as an assistant director on the monumental film Mughal-e-Azam.

Returning to the family line of Suraj Prakash Marwah: he and Sheela Marwah had four children — the eldest daughter Poonam, followed by Deepak, then Sandeep, and finally the youngest, Atul.

In Delhi, Suraj Prakash Marwah steadily laid the strong foundations of his family. It was in this environment that Sandeep Marwah spent his childhood. He received his early education at Delhi's Sardar Patel Vidyalaya, and later completed his studies at Bhagat Singh College, University of Delhi.

This background is essential to understanding Sandeep Marwah's personality. For a child raised in a family where the stories of struggle were not merely heard, but known and lived — such a child learns to see life through a different lens. A person who grows up in such an environment understands the hard work and sacrifice hidden behind every achievement, great or small.

Perhaps this is why, in Sandeep Marwah's personality, one finds empathy, an understanding of struggle, and an indomitable desire to forge ahead — all present together. Within him is not only the hunger for success, but also the memory of a legacy that had once risen, like a phoenix, from the ashes. And perhaps it is this legacy that has continued to inspire him forward — each day, each step.

2

That Schoolroom Called Childhood

Sandeep Marwah was born on 3 January 1960, in Delhi. The foundation of any person's life is laid in childhood. It is the time when the mind is most receptive, when the capacity to learn is at its greatest, and when life's first dreams begin to take shape. No matter how great a person may become later in life, the roots of their personality are almost always tied to their childhood and their education. To understand the story of Sandeep Marwah's life, it is essential to understand his childhood and his years at school.

Sandeep Marwah spent his childhood in the city of Delhi — a Delhi that was entirely different from what it is today. The city was not yet the restless, rushing place it has become. Life moved at a gentler pace, and the relationships between families carried a warmth and intimacy that was characteristic of those times. It was in this atmosphere that his childhood was slowly taking shape.

His father, Suraj Prakash Marwah, had always placed great importance on the education of his children. He understood that if his children were to get ahead in life, giving them a good education and strong values was the most essential thing of all. With this conviction, he chose one of Delhi's most respected schools for Sandeep Marwah's education — Sardar Patel Vidyalaya.

Sardar Patel Vidyalaya was, at the time, counted among the leading schools of Delhi. It paid attention not merely to academic learning, but to the all-round development of its students. This was why so many of its alumni went on to become distinguished figures in their respective fields.

Sandeep Marwah began his education at this school. From kindergarten through to Class XI, his entire school life was spent within its walls. At that time, the school had well over twelve hundred students. In such a large institution, it is no easy task for a child to carve out their own identity — yet Sandeep Marwah quickly came to understand which interests lay dormant within him.

Even in his early years at school, he had begun to sense that his interests were not confined to books alone. Theatre, art, culture, music, and activities connected with media held a particular pull for him. Whenever a cultural programme was held at school, a play was staged, or a musical activity organised, his heart was drawn in that direction.

Perhaps it was the voice of his soul, calling him towards its true path. Many children discover their passions quite late in life — but Sandeep Marwah was among those fortunate few who received an early indication of the direction their life would take.

There was also a teacher during his school years whose influence on his personality was profound and lasting. Sandeep Marwah recalls this teacher to this day with deep respect and gratitude. His name was B. V. Karanth.

B. V. Karanth taught Hindi at the school at that time. But he was far more than a classroom teacher. He was himself a gifted theatre artist and music director. His name is spoken with great reverence in the world of Indian theatre.

Sandeep Marwah had the opportunity to meet him at least twice a day — once during class lessons, and again during the school's cultural activities. Karanth sahab was not a teacher who confined himself to textbook instruction. He introduced his students to the world of art and culture as well.

He was deeply involved in the theatrical and musical activities held at school. He would teach students the nuances of acting, dialogue delivery, movement on stage, and the rhythm of music. Sandeep Marwah learned a great many important lessons about theatre and music from him.

The school's theatre group staged several plays, among them productions such as Hayavadana and Tashnagari. In these productions, senior students were generally given the principal roles. Since Sandeep Marwah was a junior at the time, the larger parts did not come his way. But this never dampened his enthusiasm for a single moment.

Whatever role he was given — however small — he performed it with complete dedication. What mattered to him was not whether the role was large or small. What filled him with joy was simply that he had been given the opportunity to stand on stage.

Even a small role was a new experience, a new exercise, and a new source of confidence.

It was also during this period that he showed a particular interest in music. While still at school, he learned to play the dhol and the tabla — the result of nearly five years of musical training.

This musical education was more than just a skill. It gave rise to a new confidence within him. He began to feel that he was capable of accomplishing something not only in academics, but in other creative fields as well.

In today's world, scoring ninety or ninety-five percent in school examinations has become relatively common. But the circumstances of that era were different. In those days, a student who scored even sixty percent was considered to have done very well.

Sandeep Marwah, too, was always serious about his studies. In his Class XI board examinations, his subjects were Hindi, English, History, Geography, and Economics. He had a particular habit that set him apart from his fellow students. Whenever a teacher taught a lesson in class, he never rested content with only that lesson. He would read ahead — studying the coming chapters before they were taught. The benefit of this was clear: by the time the teacher returned to teach the next lesson, he had already understood the material. This only deepened his grasp of the subject further.

Occasionally, his teachers would grow a little anxious observing that Sandeep Marwah's attention was being given as much to cultural activities as to his studies. They worried that these extracurricular pursuits might begin to affect his academic performance. But Sandeep Marwah maintained a balance between the two with remarkable good sense. He never let his teachers down. He remained strong in his studies while staying active in cultural life.

One incident from his school days stayed with him for a long time. When the results of his Class XI board examinations were announced, he discovered that he had missed becoming the school topper by just one mark. He had put his full effort into his studies and had hoped to secure first place. But when the final results came, he found himself one mark behind. At the time, this stung a little. But today, when he recalls that moment, he smiles. He often remembers by name the student who had secured first place that year — Anjana Bhatnagar.

With time, he came to understand that every event in life holds a meaning. What appears disappointing in the moment can, further down the road, become a source of inspiration. He often reflects that if he had received that one extra mark and become the school topper, perhaps the fire within him to keep striving would have dimmed a little. He might have allowed himself to feel complete, to stop at that achievement.

But life had far greater goals in store for him.

Alongside studies and cultural activities, sports too held a special place in his interests. He was particularly fond of volleyball and football. Running on the field, playing as part of a team, and relishing the spirit of competition gave him great pleasure. Interestingly, cricket, considered the most beloved sport in India, held no particular fascination for him.

School days are never made of studies and activities alone. They are filled with the mischief of childhood, the laughter shared with friends, and sometimes the mild jealousy that springs from friendly rivalry. Sandeep Marwah, too, lived through all of these experiences alongside his classmates. Occasionally, some peers would feel a slight envy at his level of involvement and activity. But he took all such things in his stride.

He continued to channel his energy in a positive direction. He remained a favourite among his teachers and made the most of every opportunity that came his way. He saw every school programme, every activity, and every occasion as an opportunity to learn. He participated in as many activities as he possibly could. Each experience taught him something new and added to his growing self-confidence. Gradually, a realisation began to take hold within him: that to get ahead in life, academic learning alone is not enough. Experience, art, culture, and the ability to communicate — these are equally important.

These very experiences became the strong foundation for the journey that lay ahead. Those school days — those teachers, those stages, those small roles, and those rehearsals — together, they were building the bedrock of his personality. When he later stepped onto the larger stages of life, he must surely have felt, within himself, that the confidence, the creativity, and the capacity for leadership he carried had their beginning in those very school days.

And so Sandeep Marwah's childhood was not merely the childhood of a student. It was a school in itself — one where many of life's most important lessons were learned: lessons in perseverance, in discipline, in creativity, and in the courage to keep moving forward.

3

College Days — The Time When Dreams Found Direction

There are certain junctures in life where a person does not merely study, but determines the course of their future. The period after school — the college years — is one such pivotal stage. It is the time when a young mind recognises the possibilities within itself, gives shape to its dreams, and begins to understand its relationship with the world. For Sandeep Marwah too, college was never simply a means to obtaining a degree. It was the period when his personality found a new direction altogether.

Sandeep Marwah had always been a gifted student. In recognition of his academic ability and intellectual aptitude, he had been given a double promotion during his school years, which meant he was a full year ahead of his peers. While this was an achievement in itself, it would later present an unexpected challenge. When he completed his schooling, he was only fifteen years old — old enough in ability, but not yet in the eyes of institutional rules.

At the time, the atmosphere at home was shaped by business.

The family's inclinations lay towards trade and management, and naturally, the same thoughts began to take root in Sandeep Marwah's mind as well. With this purpose, he applied to Shri Ram College of Commerce at Delhi University for B.Com Honours — an institution regarded, even then, as one of the finest in the country for commerce and management. However, the college required a minimum age of sixteen for admission, and he was still fifteen. Talent was not in question, but age stood in his way. He had to return to Sardar Patel Vidyalaya and obtain an affidavit confirming that his double promotion was the reason he was a year ahead of students his age — yet even this did not fully resolve the situation.

He made another attempt and applied to St. Stephen's College, where he was offered admission in Economics Honours — a considerable achievement given St. Stephen's reputation as one of Delhi University's most prestigious institutions. But Sandeep Marwah had already formed a clear sense of where he wanted to go: business, marketing, and management. He felt that Economics Honours would not serve that goal as directly as he needed. There was also a practical concern: St. Stephen's was on the North Campus, while his home was in Greater Kailash. The distance was considerable, and since he had always been deeply involved in cultural and extracurricular activities — often returning home late at night — his father had reservations about his safety. Though studying on the North Campus would have been a point of pride for any student, he chose, out of deference to his family, to enrol at Shaheed Bhagat Singh College on the South Campus. This decision would prove to be one of the defining choices of his life.

Delhi University at that time was as well known for student politics and agitation as it was for academics. Strikes, protests, and the activity of student organisations were commonplace. But Sandeep Marwah's nature was quite different. He was not a student drawn to politics or protest for its own sake — his faith lay in creative activity, and he wanted the college environment to be vibrant and inspiring. When he arrived, he found that the college had little by way of organised cultural life, and this troubled him. He resolved to change it by starting new clubs and activities — but this was far from simple. The college principal, Mr. Thakur, was a man of strict discipline and did not grant permission for new initiatives easily. Sandeep Marwah had to approach him multiple times, make his case patiently, and convince him that these activities would genuinely benefit the college. After persistent effort, Mr. Thakur finally agreed. Soon, several new clubs came into being — a music club, an English singing club, a Hindi singing club, and a theatre group. With their arrival, the atmosphere of the college began to transform, and the hidden talents of students began to find expression.

From the moment he joined, Sandeep Marwah made a quiet resolution: these three years would not simply pass — they would be made memorable. While most students fritter away their free hours in idle talk and aimless company, he spent his in theatre rehearsals. On the college stage, he performed in several productions, including *O Mere Sapne, Baki Itihas, and Hum Do Hamare Do*. His performances drew attention and, in time, he began to be known across the college as an outstanding actor. It was also during this period that his interest in film and television began to grow, and through professional theatre, he had the opportunity to work alongside seasoned artists including Raj Babbar, Nadira Babbar, and Anupam Kher. His reputation spread beyond his own college, and whenever cultural events were hosted by other colleges within Delhi University, Principal Mr. Thakur would personally call upon him to assemble a team and represent the college. Through these appearances, he not only carried the college's name to wider audiences but also won numerous prizes in competitions along the way.

What distinguished him, however, was never simply his individual talent. He did not build paths for himself alone — he brought others along with him. He worked through teams, believed in collective effort, and gave his peers the same opportunities he sought for himself. This quality of leadership was becoming an increasingly essential part of who he was.

Around this time, the country's political landscape underwent a dramatic shift. The declaration of Emergency under Prime Minister Indira Gandhi sent ripples across the nation, and Delhi University was no exception. Student union elections were suspended for a prolonged period. Sandeep Marwah, however, refused to let the time go to waste, channelling his energy entirely into creative pursuits. When elections eventually resumed, he decided to contest — standing for the position of Central Councillor. He threw himself into the campaign with full enthusiasm, understanding that elections are not merely a test of popularity but of organisation, communication, and leadership. He won. And when he did, he used the position not for personal gain, but in service of the college and his fellow students. He put forward a slogan — *"Help me, help yourself"* — carrying within it the simple conviction that when students support one another, they advance together, and the institution advances with them. His name began to travel across Delhi University. Among the other young people active in student politics at that time were individuals who would later become well known in their own right — including Vijay Kumar Goel, and the senior television journalist Rajat Sharma, with both of whom Sandeep Marwah worked and collaborated during those years.

His curiosity during college extended far beyond the boundaries of his own curriculum. He pursued courses in the spiritual traditions of Christianity, Hinduism, Buddhism, and Sikhism, and completed several medically oriented courses in partnership with the Red Cross Society. Over his three years at college, he undertook approximately fifteen different courses in addition to his regular studies — not to accumulate certificates, but out of a genuine desire to broaden his understanding of the world.

By the time his college years drew to a close, Sandeep Marwah was not simply a graduate. He was a young man who had, within those three years, built within himself an entire universe of confidence, experience, and aspiration — a young man who had learned leadership, teamwork, the art of communication, and the ability to recognise and seize an opportunity when it appeared. College had not merely given him a degree. It had given him a foundation — and on that foundation, he would go on to build the grand architecture of his life's work.

4

Dreams, Enterprise, and the Road of Passion

With the completion of college, a new chapter of life begins. Stepping out of the world of books, a person enters the world of reality — where each day brings a new test, a new experience, and a new opportunity to learn. Something of the same kind awaited Sandeep Marwah. Throughout his college years, his bond with theatre had remained intact, but life also holds this truth: passion alone cannot sustain a household. Employment and responsibility eventually compel a person to choose a definite path.

After earning his commerce degree, he stepped into his father's business. Suraj Prakash Marwah was a seasoned and principled businessman, and working alongside him gave Sandeep Marwah the opportunity to understand the finer workings of trade. For any son, working with his father is a particular kind of education — what books cannot teach, a father's experience often can. A father is not only a provider; he is life's first true teacher. Sandeep Marwah often speaks of his father as a man of extraordinary simplicity and contentment, someone who remained composed and steady in every circumstance, who never placed wealth above all else, and who valued humanity and relationships far more than money. One memory he returns to often captures this vividly. There came a day when his father, for some reason, did not eat. And in response, the entire household stopped eating as well. Nobody had ever seen him in such a state, and the family's collective distress spoke to the depth of feeling that bound them together. In today's world, people are often so consumed by the rush of daily life that they scarcely notice whether their parents have eaten — but in that household, each member's well-being was the concern of all. Sandeep Marwah says he is deeply grateful that the same values are visible in his own children today.

His father's manner of teaching was as distinctive as his character. Rather than explaining things outright, he preferred to put his son directly into situations and let him learn by doing. On one occasion, he wished to send Sandeep Marwah to handle an order involving an embassy. The young man was apprehensive — the responsibility felt beyond him, and he declined. But a father's instruction cannot be deferred indefinitely, and eventually he went. It was the first time in his life that he carried out a task entirely on his own, and the purpose behind it was clear: his father wanted to build confidence in his son. When a person is given a responsibility for the first time and sees it through, something new awakens within them — and so it was with Sandeep Marwah. The experience gave him the ability to speak with people, negotiate, and read a situation with clarity. He carried this lesson forward into his own role as a father, recounting how he once asked his son to sign a cheque. The boy was nervous, afraid of making a mistake, but Sandeep Marwah told him not to worry about what might go wrong — that he simply had to do it. It was the same gift his father had given him: the gift of being trusted with something real.

During their drives together, Suraj Prakash Marwah would often share stories from the world of business. His belief was firm: if a person learns to deal with retail customers well, nothing can stop them from succeeding. This philosophy had gradually transformed the family shop in Khan Market into a well-known music establishment — a place people came to not merely to buy, but to talk, to linger, and to be part of the atmosphere. Each morning, Suraj Prakash Marwah would attend to customers and manage the shop; after lunch, he would settle on the sofa for a while, and during this quiet hour, he would recount to Sandeep the conversations and encounters of the day. Through these unhurried exchanges, Sandeep Marwah developed an instinctive understanding of people — of human nature, and of what one might call the psychology of ordinary life.

In 1980, an opportunity arrived that would broaden his horizons considerably: a trip to London. Travelling abroad in those days was itself a significant occasion. The plan involved Boeing aircraft being brought to India from the United States via a London stopover, and all that was needed was a London ticket — costing around six thousand three hundred rupees. He travelled with his elder brother Deepak Marwah, and from London they obtained a Europe pass and journeyed through several countries. The vitality and orderliness of Europe left a deep impression on him. The development, the cleanliness, the systems in place — all of it made Delhi, by comparison, feel like a small town. At the time, the city still carried the marks of its slower pace of growth, though the government had begun taking meaningful steps to improve it, clearing slum settlements and constructing small flats for those who had lived there.

During his travels, he noticed something that caught his attention sharply: across many countries in Europe, there was a tremendous enthusiasm for Indian handicrafts and carpets. Wherever he went, people asked him about Indian rugs and handmade goods — admiring the artistry and craftsmanship with genuine warmth. It was in this moment that a new idea was born in his mind. On returning to India, he founded a new company which he named Continental Exports. He travelled extensively to Bhadohi, Agra, and Kashmir to understand the carpet trade from the ground up, studying the craft in genuine depth. In time, he became so knowledgeable that he could examine any carpet and tell at a glance how many knots it contained, how long it had taken to make, and where it had been woven. He would explain that a genuine silk carpet contains approximately four hundred knots per inch, woven with a silk warp and a cotton weft. A carpet that sold for around six thousand rupees in India, he discovered, could command sixty thousand abroad. Between 1982 and 1985, he traded across London, France, Switzerland, and various other European countries. His experience grew enormously during this period, though earnings — after accounting for electricity, water, salaries, and other overheads — were not as substantial as he had hoped. Nevertheless, there was a quiet satisfaction in knowing that at just twenty-three, he had already begun producing his own range of rugs, which came to be known as Sandeep Marwah Dari.

With time, he came to feel that the carpet business alone would not be sufficient to fulfil his larger ambitions, and he began looking for new avenues. He learned about the new residential colonies being developed in and around Delhi, and made contact with organisations like DLF and Ansal to understand how they operated. He realised that by helping these companies sell their plots and properties, he could earn a healthy commission — and from this point, he stepped into the world of real estate. The income was good, but the demands were considerable: clients would call early in the morning or late at night, and he often had to travel to distant sites. Despite all of this, he found real satisfaction in the work. He still remembers the day he received his first cheque of twenty-five thousand rupees, a moment that felt extraordinary, because money earned by one's own effort carries a different kind of energy. When a second cheque of fifty-five thousand rupees followed, he felt that his efforts were genuinely bearing fruit.

As his professional world expanded, so did his social one. His understanding of markets deepened, and his ability to read what customers needed grew sharper. Around this time, he also began to develop an interest in the stock market. At the Khan Market shop, conversations about stocks and trading were a frequent occurrence, and he would listen carefully, gradually absorbing the workings of the field. He started visiting the stock exchange, studying companies, shares, and the movements of the market. His time became distributed across several pursuits — real estate, exports, his father's shop, and the stock market. Yet through all of it, he never allowed his passion to die. Each evening, he would make his way to Mandi House and meet the people of the theatre world. Acting and the stage were never merely a hobby for him — they were a kind of spiritual sustenance.

Then came an incident that shook him from within. In one production, he was given an extremely minor role. He felt it was an affront to his ability — that he had become the victim of some internal politics. That day, he made a decision: he would step back from theatre. Following this, he organised his days with a clear and purposeful structure. Mornings were devoted to his father's shop, afternoons to real estate, and the remaining hours to exports and the stock market. His life remained in constant, purposeful motion.

It was also during this period that a sense of duty towards the nation stirred within him. He participated in NCC and Scout activities, and later served as Battalion Commander in the Delhi Home Guard — a position to which he was appointed by the Lieutenant Governor of Delhi of that time — serving from 1978 to 1986. In 1982, the nature of his business also brought him into regular contact with the Congress office. He became associated with the Youth Congress and had the occasion to meet Rajiv Gandhi, whose personality left a distinct impression on him — though he was careful to maintain his distance from active politics.

By now, Sandeep Marwah had begun to sense that his life's true destination still lay somewhere ahead — somewhere he had not yet arrived. Slowly, almost imperceptibly, fate was leading him towards a path where his passion, his creativity, and his accumulated experience would come together to write an entirely new story.

5

A Relationship, A Support, and Life's New Beginning

To walk the road of success, hard work, courage, and passion are essential — but for a complete and fulfilling life, a peaceful home and a thoughtful companion matter just as much. When there is a roof over one's head, a reliable means of livelihood, and genuine love and respect within the family, a quiet contentment settles into a person's life. And it is precisely this contentment that gives a person the courage to dream large and to turn those dreams into reality.

Such a moment arrived in Sandeep Marwah's life too. His business had found its footing — he had gradually established himself in real estate and the carpet trade, his hard work was bearing fruit, and his professional world was beginning to take solid shape. At such a time, it is only natural for parents to feel that their son's home should now be settled as well. His elder sister Poonam and his brother Deepak had both been married, the household was a happy one, and the family was moving forward in its own way. Sandeep Marwah recalls that in those days, his attention was entirely absorbed in building his business — he thought of little else but how to expand his trade and take it to new heights. Yet every parent holds in their heart the quiet wish that their child marry in good time and take on the responsibilities of a family. This hope must surely have lived in the heart of his father, Suraj Prakash Marwah, and in due course, conversations about prospective matches began to find their way into the household.

Several proposals came and went, but as it is often said — relationships are not formed by careful planning alone; fate has an equal hand in them. Where the match is not meant to be, no amount of effort brings it about; and where destiny has already decided, the path finds itself. Then, through a relative, a new prospect arrived — a family connected to Bombay. Both families agreed that the young man and the young woman should meet at a wedding gathering so that the conversation could move forward. But on that occasion, Sandeep Marwah was unable to arrive in time, and the meeting with Reena ji had to be postponed. Perhaps destiny simply wished to hold back the moment a little longer — for as they say, every thing has its appointed hour, and that hour is always the right one.

A day later, both families arranged to meet again, this time at the Crown Plaza in Connaught Place, Delhi — a hotel that was, at the time, owned by the well-known film producer F. C. Mehra. The two families sat together and conversation began to flow. The atmosphere was warm and easy, and before long, both sides felt that this was a match worth pursuing. Agreement was reached, and the engagement was arranged at the home of one of Reena ji's cousins, who was also acquainted with the Marwah family. Around two hundred to two hundred and fifty guests were expected, and the occasion was filled with festivity and joy. It was also at this time that they learned more about

Reena ji's family: her elder brother Boney Kapoor was a film producer, and her younger brother was trying to make his mark in the film world. He could not attend the engagement, as he had been offered a small role in a film and was away on its shoot. That film was **Shakti**, featuring two of the era's greatest artists — Dilip Kumar and Amitabh Bachchan. The young man who was absent from the celebrations that day would go on to become one of Hindi cinema's most beloved stars — known to the world today as Anil Kapoor. Reena ji's third brother, Sanjay Kapoor, also had connections to the film industry, and their father, Surendra Kapoor, was a distinguished producer and distributor of Raj Kapoor's films. This union, then, was not merely a meeting of two families — it was also a new bridge between two very different worlds: business and cinema. Among the distinguished guests who came from Bombay for the engagement were Krishna Raj Kapoor, Reema Kapoor, and Champu Kapoor, bound together not only by family ties but by genuine warmth and friendship. Actors Dharmendra and Om Prakash were also present at the wedding. The entire ceremony unfolded with simplicity and heartfelt intimacy.

The match was settled in 1982, and the very next year, in 1983, Reena Kapoor became Reena Marwah and entered Sandeep Marwah's life as his companion. It is often said that behind every successful man stands a woman — and now that hand had come to rest gently on his shoulder. A new chapter of his life was about to begin: one in which family, responsibility, and the pursuit of dreams would walk forward together.

Reflecting on those early years, Sandeep Marwah sometimes smiles and says that his wife's life was no different from that of a soldier's wife. He spent most of his time away from home on account of work. Any newly married woman naturally wishes to spend as much time as possible with her husband, to share in the small joys of daily life — yet Reena ji never complained. She accepted circumstances with patience and understanding, and built the home with quiet strength. Sandeep Marwah also recalls how his father, Suraj Prakash Marwah, looked after Reena ji with the same care a father shows his daughter — she was always held with affection and respect within the family. He adds another detail that speaks volumes about his father's character: Suraj Prakash Marwah never once travelled abroad. He left that privilege entirely for his children, believing that if the next generation moved forward and flourished, that would be his greatest achievement. In a home where every member feels the weight of their duties more than the pull of their rights, life does indeed become something like paradise.

Sandeep Marwah never attributes his success to his own efforts alone. He often says that the contributions of his wife, his mother, and his sisters have been among the most significant forces in his life. In his own words: "There are three women in my life whom I have always held sacred — my mother, my wife, and my sister." He believes deeply that every woman in the world is deserving of respect — that within a woman lies a remarkable depth of dedication, patience, and love. It is perhaps this conviction that led him, in the years that followed, to take numerous initiatives in support of women's honour and empowerment — organising webinars and seminars, and founding recognitions such as the Sarojini Naidu Award, so that the contributions of women to society might be acknowledged and their self-confidence strengthened. His belief is firm: when women are given opportunity and respect, the whole of society grows stronger.

He also places great emphasis on the importance of connecting the younger generation with the older one — that today's youth carry energy and fresh ideas, while those who have lived longer carry experience and wisdom, and that if the two generations learn from each other, the progress of society can be far swifter and more meaningful. This conviction continues to inspire him to serve as a bridge between the young and the old.

And so, in Sandeep Marwah's life, marriage was never merely a family event. It brought with it stability, companionship, and a new kind of energy. It was the turning point from which his dreams would take a higher flight — and perhaps it was this peaceful foundation that gave him, in the years ahead, the strength to turn even the grandest of dreams into reality.

6

A Dream That Became Noida's Identity

Driven by his passion for theatre and acting, Sandeep Marwah also tried his luck in films — though whether one calls it fortune or misfortune, he worked in three films, none of which were ever released. What troubled him most was not the outcome itself, but the process: for even a small role, he would have to sit for hours in makeup, waiting for his moment on set. Gradually, the feeling took hold within him that something larger was waiting for him elsewhere. He made up his mind to leave Bombay.

When he returned from Bombay in 1982, there was a particular restlessness in his heart — not the restlessness of failure, but of someone who needs to create, to build something new. He had always believed that time is not merely meant to be passed; it is meant to be used well, and that those who truly understand time are the ones who eventually make history. His connection with theatre continued as before, and the world of the stage never ceased to draw him — the lights, the energy of performers, the sound of an audience's applause were all deeply close to his heart. But alongside this love for the stage, there lived another, older pull: the camera. The idea of standing behind a lens and capturing a moment, recording a story as a visual scene, had always excited him. It was this feeling that gave birth to a new thought: why not begin something that belonged to the world of the camera and of news? And so, following that instinct, he started a news agency in Delhi's Khan Market.

The world of that era was entirely unlike the digital age of today. Doordarshan was the country's principal television medium, and the cameras it used were known, half in jest, as relics from another age altogether. Technology was severely limited and the work operated along governmental lines. Sandeep Marwah's news agency, however, possessed the most advanced cameras available at the time — lighter, sharper, and superior in quality. Word gradually spread, and the agency began to be called upon to cover significant events. Orders came in for coverage of programmes involving the Prime Minister, the President, and several major national figures. This work introduced him to the world of news and current affairs, and he came to understand that the camera is not merely an instrument of entertainment — it is a powerful means of recording history. He recalls that in those days, he would often carry heavy camera equipment to events himself, working late into the night or setting out early in the morning for a morning assignment. But he never considered any task too small or too large. His conviction was firm: work done with genuine heart becomes life's greatest teacher. Through this work, the craft of filmmaking began to reveal itself to him — the angle of a shot, the use of light, the way a scene is recorded — all of it slowly settling into his understanding. He could not have known then that this very experience was preparing him for the most significant project of his life.

After nearly two years in this work, a larger idea began to form in his mind. If this could be taken to a greater scale, he realised, it could be not merely a passion but a serious enterprise. And so, in 1986, a dream began to take shape — bold, specific, and unprecedented. If Bombay could be home to a glittering film industry, why could a similar centre not be built near Delhi? Noida at that time was nothing like the developed city it has since become; there was silence and open land as far as the eye could see. But where others saw emptiness, Sandeep Marwah saw possibility. In that quietness, just a short distance from Delhi, he began to envision a new film city.

At just twenty-six years of age, he prepared a detailed project file and set out to make it a reality. He went first to the Land and Development Office, hoping that officials there would understand his vision and show him the way forward. Instead, he was discouraged. He carried his file from one office to the next, visiting the MCD as well, and met with the same dismissiveness at every turn. People in the Delhi-NCR region had little familiarity with cinema or the film industry. At the time, the only two organised channels of entertainment were All India Radio on Parliament Street and Doordarshan — both government institutions and both difficult to access. It was in this period that Sandeep Marwah arrived at a deeper understanding: anyone who wishes to bring something new into the world must, like Shiva, be prepared to swallow a great deal of poison. People will call them foolish; they will laugh at their dreams. But it is the ones who persevere through all of this — who labour with the determination of Bhagirath — who ultimately write history. Sandeep Marwah was never going to be one of those who stopped.

As fate would have it, the well-known music shop his family ran in Khan Market was a gathering place for music lovers and senior officials alike. One day, by chance, the Chairman of the Noida Authority happened to visit the shop. In the course of conversation, he learned of the film city project. He listened with genuine interest and invited Sandeep Marwah to come to his office. When the meeting took place some days later, it was the first time Sandeep Marwah felt that a government official was truly grasping the depth of his vision. Noida was a new city at the time, without a distinct identity of its own, and the authorities themselves were aware that a landmark project could give it one. The idea of a film city struck the Chairman as genuinely compelling, and he suggested that the project be finalised and sent to Lucknow. The Chief Minister of Uttar Pradesh at the time was Veer Bahadur Singh — a man with a particular fondness for cinema — and when the proposal reached him, he too was enthusiastic. The file was sent to Lucknow in December 1986, and Sandeep Marwah returned to his regular work. Nearly a year later, in December 1987, word came that the project had been approved. He could scarcely believe it. In his own words: *"It was as if the dreams had come true."*

The process of land allocation for the film city in Noida now began, and Sandeep Marwah travelled to Bombay to meet with prominent figures from the industry. Gradually, several major names agreed to associate themselves with the project — among them Boney Kapoor, Danny Denzongpa, Prakash Mehra, Kamleshwar, and Gulshan Kumar. Their involvement lent the project a new credibility. The question of location then had to be decided, and Sandeep Marwah chose Sector

16A. The area was utterly deserted at the time, and Noida Authority officials found the choice amusing, suggesting instead that the already-developed industrial area of Sector 6 would be far more practical. But he held his ground. A film city, he argued, requires a calm environment — open land, and the presence of a river nearby. The Yamuna flowed close to that spot, and the surrounding silence was exactly what he was looking for. His foresight proved sound. Land allocation began in 1988, and people began to come on board. Gulshan Kumar showed interest and brought several other producers along. Construction of Marwah Studios commenced, and Sandeep Marwah continued reaching out to filmmakers, directors, and artists, inviting them to work at the studios.

In March 1988, when the formal land allocation took place, a grand ceremony was organised. Thousands gathered at the site, and several artists made the journey from Mumbai to attend. But on that very day, an unfortunate event cast a shadow over the occasion — Sandeep Marwah's paternal grandfather-in-law passed away, and he had to leave immediately for Mumbai. When he returned three or four days later, he found his name printed in the newspapers alongside some of the most celebrated figures in the country. He wrote in his diary: *"Today I feel I have done something for this nation."* Perhaps that was the very moment when one young man's dream had become a city's identity.

7

A Devotee of Time and an Architect of Dreams

In all the time I have observed Sandeep Marwah up close, one thing has always been clear — he is never idle. He is either doing something or thinking of something new. For him, time is not merely the movement of clock hands; it is the capital of life itself, and he accounts for every moment of it. Many people remark on how extraordinarily active he is, but it seems to me that activity is not something he practises — it is simply his nature. To be always doing, always creating, has become not a habit but a philosophy of living.

In those days, Delhi and the surrounding region were known for administrative and commercial activity, not for the film industry. But where others see the impossible, certain people see possibility — and Sandeep Marwah saw possibility. Once the film city project received approval, work began in earnest. He threw himself into designing and bringing the vision to life: studios, outdoor locations, technical facilities — every aspect was attended to with meticulous care. His purpose was clear: to give the Mumbai film industry a strong and credible alternative in northern India. He reached out to well-known figures from the profession, and gradually several prominent names established their studios in Noida Film City — Boney Kapoor, Padmini Kolhapuri, Danny, Prakash Mehra, and many others. The shared belief was that a fully developed film industry could indeed be built here.

Sandeep Marwah spared nothing in his efforts and brought the project to life with complete dedication. But every dream needs more than structures and resources — it needs the commitment of people. In the professional environment of Delhi-NCR, that collective will and the kind of devotion to cinema that one finds in Mumbai was not easy to sustain. Many saw it primarily as a business proposition rather than an artistic endeavour, and as a result, progress did not come at the pace that had been hoped for. With time, circumstances began to shift. Some grew disillusioned. Talk began to circulate — that films would never really be made here, that the studios might eventually be put to some other use, that they would end up as grain warehouses. Such conversations could have broken the spirit of any visionary. But Sandeep Marwah held his ground. He faced the difficult period with the same seriousness with which he had faced the good times, and he did not allow his enthusiasm to wane.

His experiences in Mumbai had already taught him something important. In those days, any artist who wished to be taken seriously in the film industry was expected to have trained at the Film and Television Institute of India in Pune. Each stream there had only about ten seats — while thousands of young people carried dreams of making it in cinema. Countless talented individuals were unable to pursue their ambitions simply because opportunity was so scarce. Sandeep

Marwah recognised this not as a problem but as an opening. Why not establish, in northern India, a private film institution that could offer professional training to young people? The idea was audacious for its time — the concept of film education in the private sector was virtually non-existent. And then, at precisely this juncture, something else occurred that strengthened his resolve: India's liberalisation policy opened the door for twenty-four-hour news channels, and with that came the obvious question of where the skilled manpower to run them would come from. The television industry was growing rapidly, and it would need trained professionals. His mind was made up. It was out of this thinking that India's first private media institution — the Asian Academy of Film and Television — was born.

The early days were anything but easy. Limited resources, the search for trained faculty, the challenge of convincing young people that this institution could genuinely shape their futures — every step presented its own difficulty. He himself often quotes the old Hindi saying — "Kaheen ki eent, kaheen ka roda, Bhanumati ne kunba joda" — meaning that things were pieced together from wherever they could be found. And that is precisely what happened: people came from different directions, some contributed equipment, some experience, some their time. Slowly, a team was formed, a structure took shape, and what had begun as one man's conviction grew into something resembling a movement. Many regarded the effort as swimming against the current — the film industry's heart was in Mumbai, and to lay a serious foundation for film education and production in northern India seemed extraordinary. But Sandeep Marwah was resolute. His stubbornness was not of the negative kind — it was the stubbornness of creation: the insistence on doing something new, on keeping pace with the times, and on treating time itself with respect.

His daily life is proof of this. From early morning to late at night, he remains active — meetings, classes, events, plans — and he is personally present in all of it. He is not an administrator who merely gives directions; he is a leader who participates. Perhaps this is why the institution became not merely a collection of buildings but a living, breathing family. Over time, the Asian Academy of Film and Television built a name for itself not only across northern India but nationally and internationally. Thousands of students trained here and went on to work across the media landscape — some making their mark in acting, some in direction, some in journalism, some in the technical fields. A dream that had once seemed confined to the boundaries of Mumbai was now taking root in the soil of Noida.

When I look back at his journey, one thread runs clearly through it all: respect for time. The waiting in Mumbai taught him never to let time go to waste. Returning to Delhi and realising the film city dream, holding firm through difficulty, and then charting a new course in education — through all of this, the understanding of time's value is unmistakable. He often says that if you keep doing, the path will keep forming — and perhaps that is why he is never seen at rest. For him, stillness means moving backward. He believes that life requires momentum, but that momentum must be purposeful.

Today, when people speak of Noida Film City and Marwah Studios, they speak of an established name. But behind that name lies a long story of struggle, setbacks, criticism, and unrelenting effort. Sandeep Marwah did not merely build structures — he gave form to a vision. He is a devotee of time, meeting each moment with full attention and recognising each opportunity as it arises. And he is an architect of dreams, taking raw ideas and giving them solid form. His journey teaches that failure is never an ending — it is a signal to change direction. If Mumbai gave him the lesson of patience, Delhi gave him the opportunity to build. His story also reminds us that dreaming requires courage, but turning dreams into reality requires discipline and a deep respect for time. Sandeep Marwah has mastered both — and perhaps that is why his life remains in perpetual motion: always doing, always thinking, and always making time meaningful.

8

A Living Example of Relentless Effort — Dr. Sandeep Marwah

There are certain personalities in the world about whom the word "hardworking" feels like an understatement — a description that does not do justice to their true stature. To understand such lives, one needs words like "relentless," "unceasing," "passionate," and "self-driven." These are people who are known by their work, and whose identity is built not from any single achievement but from a lifetime of continuous striving. Dr. Sandeep Marwah is one such person, not merely a professional, but a living embodiment of what diligence looks like. His life is proof that when a person's resolve is strong, they can turn their dreams into reality.

I have had the privilege of observing him closely and working alongside him, and everything I say about him here is not drawn from ceremonial praise or hearsay, but from direct experience. I have watched him work, felt his energy, and come to understand that for him, work is not simply a profession — it is the purpose of life itself. Hard work is woven into his very nature. He is not the kind of person who defers tasks or leaves them to others. His belief is that the sooner a task is begun, the better, and for him, work is not a burden but a source of both responsibility and joy. This is why he never regards any task as too small or too large. There have been countless occasions — a programme in preparation, chairs to be arranged, tables to be set, a stage to be readied — when rather than directing others, he has simply stepped forward and begun the work himself. To watch him do this, without ceremony and without ego, is itself an education. In an age when many people believe leadership means giving instructions, Sandeep Marwah leads by example. This is precisely what sets him apart.

Among the greatest achievements of his life is the realisation of his dream to establish a film city in northern India — a vision that many, when he first put it forward, considered nothing more than fantasy. But he did not allow it to remain a dream. He made it a resolve, and then worked tirelessly to honour that resolve. Noida Film City is a recognised name today, but behind it lie years of effort, struggle, and patience. Bringing any large project to the ground requires plans to be drawn, officials to be met, long bureaucratic processes to be navigated, and disappointment to be absorbed. Sandeep Marwah faced all of this without ever surrendering. Getting the project approved by the Noida Authority, shaping its blueprint, finalising its design, and turning it into something real — he stood at the centre of all of it. This was not the work of a day or a month. It was the result of years of uninterrupted effort.

Every great work begins with a small first step. For Sandeep Marwah, that first step was Marwah Studios — the place where the foundation of his larger vision was laid. Despite limited resources, he demonstrated that if the thinking is clear and the effort genuine, even the impossible can be made possible. Marwah Studios did not remain merely a studio; it became a centre of creativity, a place from which countless artists, technicians, and students found the opportunity to learn and grow. Over time, it became a source of inspiration for all those who wished to build their future in the worlds of media and film.

From there, he took an equally significant step into the field of education. The Asian Academy of Film and Television was not simply an institution — it was an idea: the idea of creative education. His purpose was unambiguous: not to give young people a degree, but to give them the skills to realise their own dreams. He believed that education must not be confined to books — it must be practical, connected to life, and responsive to the changing times. Today, the Asian Academy of Film and Television has built a name for itself not just across India but around the world. Thousands of students who trained here are now working in film, media, television, and digital platforms. All of this is the result of one person's foresight and hard work. But his journey did not stop there. He went on to establish the Asian School of Media Studies, and today approximately sixteen schools operate under the AAFT name. Beyond this, a full university — AAFT University of Media and Arts, dedicated to film and media and recognised by the University Grants Commission — stands on twenty-seven acres in Raipur, Chhattisgarh. This makes it clear that his vision was never limited to a single institution. He wanted to give every field of media a strong and enduring foundation, driven by the conviction that if young people receive the right guidance and opportunity, they have the power to bring about genuine change in society.

What further distinguishes him is his attitude towards work itself. I have never once heard him say that things will move when someone shows up to make them move. He does not wait for others. If a team is present, he works with the team; if it is not, he begins alone. He holds that true leadership is not the giving of orders but the willingness to be first. This is precisely why his team works with full dedication and enthusiasm — because his leadership speaks through action, not through words. The organisation of over eight thousand five hundred events to date is, in itself, an extraordinary achievement. Each event brings its own challenges — a new plan, a new team, a new set of pressures — yet Sandeep Marwah approaches each one with the same energy as if it were his first. He involves himself personally in every preparation, his attention touching everything from the decoration of the stage to the precise running order of the programme. This commitment is what makes him exceptional. And it is not only in events but in writing that his activity is equally remarkable: he has authored over seven thousand five hundred news articles and pieces to date — a number that is not merely a statistic but a testament to his unbroken engagement with the world. For him, writing is not simply a form of expression; it is a way of being in conversation with society. His words carry the depth of lived experience, and it is this that gives them their power.

For nearly forty years, he has worked continuously — without pause, without fatigue. This constancy is his greatest asset. In an age when people seek rapid success, Sandeep Marwah's life teaches us that real success comes through time, patience, and earnest effort. He does not merely speak about success — he shows the way to it. His life is not only a story of achievements; it is an inspiration. It tells us that when the intention is strong and the effort is honest, no dream is beyond reach.

When we look at the life of Dr. Sandeep Marwah today, it is evident that he is more than a name. He is an idea — the idea of hard work, the idea of continuity, and the idea of self-reliant leadership. His journey is an inspiration for the generations to come, and particularly for those young people who carry large dreams but are still searching for the path. His life sends them a message: if there is belief in the heart and the steps do not stop, every dream can one day be made real. Dr. Sandeep Marwah is, in the truest sense, a synonym for perseverance — a person for whom work is worship, and whose life teaches that there is no substitute for relentless effort.

9

A Pioneer of Media Education in India and the World

In the rapidly evolving world of media and communication, where technology and creativity together shape global narratives, the role of visionary educators becomes profoundly important. Very few personalities have not only understood this transformation but actively given it direction. Sandeep Marwah stands out as one such pioneering figure. His contribution to media education, whether in India or at the international level, is not merely institutional, it is transformative, far-reaching, and deeply influential.

There was a time when media education in India was in its infancy, confined largely to theoretical frameworks and limited practical experience. It was in this context that Sandeep Marwah envisioned a robust and dynamic educational system — one where learning would be practical, industry-oriented, and globally connected. Guided by this vision, the Asian Academy of Film and Television was established in 1993, going on to become one of the most influential media training institutions in the country.

The Asian Academy of Film and Television was not merely an educational institution — it was a revolution in media education. It adopted a hands-on approach in which students were not simply learners but creators. Through real studios, live projects, and continuous interaction with industry professionals, students gained an experience that had previously been unavailable in India. Over the years, AAFT trained thousands of students from around the world, transforming itself into an international centre for media education.

Building on this strong foundation, Sandeep Marwah further expanded his vision through the Asian Education Group, under which sixteen specialised institutions now operate. These institutions cover a wide range of creative and professional fields, collectively presenting a comprehensive educational ecosystem in the areas of media, arts, and management.

Among the most remarkable achievements of this journey is the establishment of AAFT University of Media and Arts. Located in Raipur, Chhattisgarh, this UGC-recognised university represents a significant milestone in Indian media education — marking the transition from private training institutes to a full-fledged academic university, one that offers degree programmes while placing special emphasis on practical learning. Balancing traditional academic discipline with the demands of modern industry, it prepares students for the challenges of the global media landscape.

The diversity of disciplines within the Asian Education Group reflects Marwah's comprehensive understanding of media and the creative industries. The AAFT School of Cinema provides intensive training in filmmaking, direction, cinematography, and production, nurturing storytellers who go on to create compelling cinema and digital content. The AAFT

School of Journalism and Mass Communication equips students with the skills essential for modern journalism — including digital reporting, broadcasting, and media ethics.

Recognising the growing importance of visual arts and aesthetics, institutions such as the AAFT School of Fashion and Design and the AAFT School of Interior Design focus on developing creativity for the design and fashion industries. These schools combine artistic vision with technical proficiency to prepare students for global competition.

Keeping pace with the demands of the digital age, Marwah has consistently ensured that his institutions remain ahead of their time. The AAFT School of Digital Marketing offers specialisation in online branding, social media strategy, and digital analytics, while the AAFT School of Animation and the AAFT School of Still Photography provide advanced training in visual storytelling through modern techniques.

Understanding the interconnections between media and other industries, he extended his educational efforts into diverse fields. The AAFT School of Hospitality and Tourism prepares students for the global tourism and service industry, while the AAFT School of Health and Wellness focuses on emerging sectors related to health and lifestyle. Acknowledging the central role of communication and brand management in modern business, the AAFT School of Advertising, PR and Events trains professionals capable of managing public perception and large-scale events effectively. The Asian Business School and Asian Law College further broaden the scope by extending into management and legal education, encouraging interdisciplinary study.

Among the most forward-thinking initiatives under this educational umbrella is AAFT Online — a reflection of Marwah's adaptability to changing educational trends. Through its online courses, it breaks through geographical barriers and makes quality media education accessible to students across the world.

What distinguishes Sandeep Marwah's contribution most powerfully is not the number of institutions, but the philosophy that binds them together. His educational approach is grounded in experiential learning, global exposure, and continuous innovation. Through international collaborations, student exchange programmes, and global film festivals, he has built a strong bridge between India and the world.

Students from more than one hundred and forty-five countries have been part of this educational ecosystem, making it one of the most diverse platforms in media education. This multicultural environment enriches the learning process and simultaneously prepares students to work at the international level — making his institutions true global ambassadors of Indian education.

Another significant dimension of his contribution is the strong connection with industry. By integrating real projects, internships, and live productions into the curriculum, he ensures that students emerge not merely with a degree but with experience and confidence. This model has expanded employment opportunities and established a benchmark for other institutions to follow.

Beyond this, Sandeep Marwah has consistently championed the idea that media education must not be limited to technical skills alone. It must incorporate values, social responsibility, and cultural awareness. Through various platforms, workshops, and community initiatives, his institutions inspire students to use media as an instrument of positive change.

In a country as diverse as India, where the tradition of storytelling runs very deep, his work has played a vital role in giving these narratives a modern and global form. By providing young creators with a platform, he has empowered a new generation that is today making its contribution to the global media landscape.

His efforts at the international level have been equally impactful. Through collaborations with foreign universities, participation in global events, and engagement with international organisations, he has secured a meaningful place for India in the world of media education. These efforts have not only attracted international students but also opened doors of global opportunity for Indian students.

Ultimately, Sandeep Marwah's contribution to media education is both vast and far-reaching. He has not merely built institutions — he has developed an educational system that nurtures creativity, innovation, and excellence. His work has transformed the character and presentation of media education, both in India and across the world.

Today, as the world moves rapidly towards an age built on content, communication, and creativity, the importance of such visionary leadership only grows greater. Sandeep Marwah's legacy is not confined to the present, it is a significant step in shaping the future of global storytelling.

10

A Synonym for Commitment

There are certain personalities who are known not by their work but by their conduct — defined not by their position, their achievements, or the events they organise, but by their commitment, the honesty of their word, and the dignity with which they honour a promise. Dr. Sandeep Marwah is one such person. His contribution to media, culture, literature, and education is as wide as his sense of values is deep. I have observed him across many platforms and in many circumstances, but one incident remains with me above all others — one that continues to remind me of the height of his character.

Dr. Sandeep Marwah has given the country four major festivals: the Global Film Festival, the Global Journalism Festival, the Global Literary Festival, and the Global Fashion Week. It is the Global Literary Festival that I wish to speak about from personal experience. We have been organising it continuously since 2015, and it is no ordinary event. To keep such a gathering — a confluence of literature, journalism, cinema, art, and ideas — alive year after year, to give it fresh energy each time and preserve its dignity, is itself a significant undertaking. Eleven editions have now been successfully completed, and with each passing year, the festival has grown more mature, more expansive, and more impactful. This very continuity is the first proof of his commitment. The Global Literary Festival is not merely a literary platform — it is a dialogue of ideas. Here, words are not only read but felt. The stage belongs not only to writers but to the issues that society most often pushes to the margins: women's empowerment, social equality, creative freedom — these become not merely topics of discussion but centres of genuine feeling. And it is this vision that elevates Dr. Sandeep Marwah from an organiser to a thoughtful leader.

One incident from 2017 stands out in my memory as being particularly revealing of his character. During that year's Global Literary Festival, a book titled Can I To I Can was to be formally launched — a collection of the life stories of approximately twenty-five women. It was a significant occasion in itself. All the women whose stories appeared in the book were present in person, and many more had been invited. Around eighty women filled the hall that day, and the atmosphere was alive with anticipation and excitement. Then, on that very same day, an urgent and unavoidable meeting was suddenly scheduled for Dr. Sandeep Marwah — the kind that is not easy to postpone. For most people in such a situation, the natural response would be to hand the programme over to someone else, or to offer a formal apology for their absence. Dr. Sandeep Marwah did neither. He asked me to address the assembled women from the stage and assured me that he would conclude his meeting and reach as quickly as he possibly could.

I went up to the stage and began — speaking about women's empowerment, about the struggles the book documented, about the role of women in society, and about the significance of what had been compiled in those pages. I spoke with full sincerity, and the women in the hall listened with close attention. Time passed. I elaborated on the themes, added examples, shared reflections. But gradually, I felt that I had said what I had to say, and yet the time kept moving. Dr. Sandeep Marwah had still not arrived. By now nearly an hour and a half had gone by, and my own restlessness was beginning to grow. The greatest fear for any speaker on stage is that they will begin to repeat themselves — and I was approaching that point. I was sending him messages on my phone between sentences, hoping for some indication of when he might arrive, but there was no definite answer. A person on stage may appear composed to the audience, but inwardly they are fighting a quiet battle — and that is precisely what I was doing.

What was equally remarkable was the patience of the women seated in that hall. They were waiting — not for a formality, but for the person in whose name they had come. That waiting was, in itself, an act of faith. And faith, as it happens, is never wasted. After roughly an hour and a half, Dr. Sandeep Marwah walked into the hall. The moment he entered, the atmosphere shifted. It was not simply the arrival of an organiser — it was the arrival of a man who had made a promise and kept it. He went directly to the stage. There was no formal apology, no lengthy explanation. The very first words he spoke, as he took his place at the podium, have stayed with me ever since:

"Raghukal reet sada chali aayi, praan jaye par vachan na jaayi."

(The code of the Raghu clan has always held: a life may be given, but a promise never broken.)

The hall erupted in applause. It was not merely a quotation — it was a declaration: of commitment, of values, and of the honour in which a word must be held. In that single moment, an hour and a half of waiting became meaningful. The look of quiet fulfilment on the faces of the women present is something I find difficult to put into words. The speech that followed was no formal address. It was drawn from experience, filled with feeling, and offered as a tribute to the courage of every woman in that book. He praised the work itself, but he also saluted the bravery of each individual who had contributed to it. He made it felt that this stage was not merely an event — it was an act of honouring women's voices.

Every woman in that hall left feeling that her presence had been worthwhile. The patience with which they had waited had been repaid. The wait had not become a burden — it had become a positive memory. This is among Dr. Sandeep Marwah's greatest qualities: the ability to take any situation and, through his sensitivity and the power of his words, turn it into something meaningful. That day taught me that commitment is not simply a matter of arriving on time. Commitment means binding one's word to one's deepest values. For Dr. Sandeep Marwah, a stage is not a formal obligation — it is a moral responsibility. He understands that people come not merely to attend an event but carrying trust, and that to keep that trust unbroken is his real success.

Even within the world of media, he has never compromised on human values. His commitment does not end at the boundary of an event — it extends to every person who connects with him. This is why writers, artists, students, and women from all walks of life regard him with genuine respect. His life teaches that great achievements are built not through plans alone, but through character. His personality is proof that when words and actions become one, a person becomes not merely successful but trustworthy.

This chapter offers only a glimpse of his life, but within this single incident, his entire philosophy is visible — a philosophy of promise, of faith, and of commitment. And perhaps this is precisely why Dr. Sandeep Marwah is not merely a media personality, but a person of lasting worth.

11

Respect as an Identity

A person's true identity is not determined by their position, their achievements, or their fame, but by how they treat others. This is something I have come to understand deeply through my years of working with Dr. Sandeep Marwah. My association with him spans nearly fifteen years, and in that time I have observed him in many different roles — as a media leader, as an organiser, as an educator, and above all as a person of deep feeling. Across all these roles, one quality has always remained constant: respect.

I have never seen Dr. Sandeep Marwah treat any person as lesser or greater than another. For him, there is no distinction between the important and the unimportant, the wealthy and the modest, the new employee and the long-standing colleague. His manner with everyone — men and women alike — is equally gracious and considerate. This is not a performance; it is simply who he is. And it is precisely this quality that makes every person who meets him feel genuinely valued. His regard for women, in particular, is deeply cultured and thoughtful. I have observed on many occasions that when a woman comes to meet him, he engages with her through the entire conversation with full attentiveness and respect, and when the meeting concludes, he does not merely offer a formal farewell — he rises from his chair and walks her to the door of his office himself. It is a small gesture, but its effect is profound. It communicates, without a word, that the person before him is not simply a visitor but someone deserving of honour. He invariably asks whether tea or coffee would be welcome, whether there is anything that might be causing discomfort. These habits have, over time, become part of my own life as well. I freely acknowledge that I learned this particular grace from him — that working alongside him taught me not only professional skills but the finer nuances of human conduct.

From my own experience, I can say without hesitation that Dr. Sandeep Marwah is a person of genuine refinement. The humility within him did not come from any training — it emerged from his deepest values. And this humility elevates him rather than diminishing him. In this regard, one incident has remained alive in my memory ever since, and it deepened my respect for him many times over.

The occasion was a distinguished event held at the FICCI auditorium in New Delhi. Well-known figures from across the country were present — prominent personalities from various fields and ambassadors from several nations. The atmosphere was formal and dignified, of the kind where people tend to be keenly aware of their own standing and position. During the programme, my eye fell on a familiar figure: Padma Shri Sheila Jhunjhunwala, the former editor of the weekly Hindustan. I hold her in the deepest respect. She must have been around ninety-five years of age at the time — she is ninety-nine today.

I knew her personally and had visited her home on several occasions. Her personality, her writing, and her life had always been a source of inspiration for me. When an opportunity arose during the event, I went with Dr. Sandeep Marwah to greet her. As I have always done, I touched her feet in the traditional gesture of reverence — not as a formality, but as an expression of my own values.

What happened next shook something within me. Without any hesitation, Dr. Sandeep Marwah stepped forward and touched her feet as well. I confess I simply stood watching him for a few moments. I had not expected it. It is commonly observed that when a person reaches a certain height — when position, prestige, and achievement accumulate — an unspoken pride tends to follow. Such a person begins, often without realising it, to place themselves above others. But in that moment, Dr. Sandeep Marwah shattered this assumption entirely. Surrounded by dignitaries and ambassadors and celebrated figures, in the midst of one of Delhi's most formal gatherings, he bent before an elderly woman of learning and made something perfectly clear: that for him, respect is not tied to a person's rank, but to their age and experience. It was not merely a physical gesture — it was a deep cultural and human statement. He demonstrated, in that single act, that true greatness lies in the willingness to bow, not in the stiffness of pride.

That one moment deepened my regard for him in a way that is difficult to articulate. I understood that Dr. Sandeep Marwah is not simply a fine speaker on a stage — he is a man who lives by his values. His conduct makes clear that however high he has risen, and to whatever level he now belongs, he has arrived there without leaving his roots behind. From that day, I no longer see him merely as a senior professional or an influential media figure. I see him as a person who lives, in the fullest sense, the foundational qualities of Indian culture — respect, humility, and gratitude.

Over the fifteen years of this journey together, I have watched many people come and go. Many faces changed, many behaviours changed, and many people's character shifted as success arrived. But Dr. Sandeep Marwah's nature never changed. His sense of respect remained constant and stable, whether the person before him was a new student or a distinguished guest of national stature. This is the quality that makes him truly singular. He understands that genuine leadership does not come from giving instructions, but from the way one conducts oneself — and when a leader himself offers respect, the entire atmosphere around him fills with it.

His life is proof that success and values are not opposites. They can walk together. In fact, the deeper truth is that it is precisely those who do not abandon their values who continue to be held in lasting regard. This chapter is not merely an account of one experience — it is a record of a value. The value of respect. And its living example is Dr. Sandeep Marwah.

12

A Personality Standing Between Laughter, Life, and Pressure

There are certain people whose very presence transforms a room. They walk in, and with them walks an energy, a vitality that fills the air. Dr. Sandeep Marwah is one such person. To see him only as a media leader, an educator, or an institution builder would be to understand him incompletely. Within him lives a human, spontaneous, and wonderfully humorous side that makes him all the more real — all the more one's own.

The responsibilities that fill his life are considerable: running multiple institutions, facing new challenges every day, staying in conversation with people across the country and the world. None of this is easy. He often says himself that if he did not approach life with a certain lightness and laughter, stress would overwhelm him. Perhaps this is why he keeps his sense of humour alive and well. His belief is that laughter is not merely entertainment — it is a necessity for maintaining mental balance. There are moments when his playfulness reaches such heights that those around him are left helpless with laughter. His stories, his expressions, his impromptu performances — everything is so natural that the listener is not watching someone entertain them, but feels as though life itself has begun to speak. Two small incidents come to mind that beautifully illuminate this vivid, humorous side of him.

The first took place in a small hall at Marwah Studios, where a book launch had been organised for a woman author. The atmosphere was entirely literary — writers, poets, thinkers, and people connected to the arts had gathered. I was seated there, as was the well-known Mumbai film director Ashok Tyagi. The launch went wonderfully: the stage saw thoughtful conversation, serious discussion about the book, and generous appreciation for the author. Afterwards, there was the customary arrangement of tea and samosas, and everyone settled into the lighter, informal mood that follows such occasions. As I have come to know of him, Dr. Sandeep Marwah never lets an opportunity for conversation pass, whether the setting is a formal stage or an informal tea table — and that day was no different. Everyone was sharing their thoughts when Ashok Tyagi, true to his particular style, began speaking over others. He has a habit of ensuring his words find their way into any conversation regardless of who is speaking, and he started in with his characteristic "main... main... meri baat suno..." — cutting into what Dr. Sandeep Marwah was saying. At that point, Marwah ji had just finished his samosa and was holding a tissue paper, in the middle of making his point with full concentration. Without missing a beat, and without uttering a single word, he quietly rolled the tissue into a ball and proceeded to mime stuffing it into his own mouth — as if to say, "Very well, I suppose I'll just stop talking then." The gesture was so unexpected, so perfectly timed, that everyone in the room dissolved into laughter. Ashok Tyagi himself looked sheepish, understanding immediately that he had been rather too overbearing. With that one silent act, Dr. Sandeep Marwah had resolved the entire situation — without a trace of bitterness, without a hint of embarrassment to anyone. This is his gift: he uses humour not as a weapon, but as a means of restoring balance.

The second incident is even more delightful, and even now, when it returns to me, I find myself laughing. One day I was sitting with Dr. Sandeep Marwah, deep in discussion on some matter, when his PA came in to inform him that someone had arrived to meet him. He asked, quite naturally, who it was. She replied that the person knew him. "Send them in," he said. A moment later, the visitor entered and, without any preamble, announced: "You looking same only. Before also handsome, now also same." He was South Indian, and his Hindi carried that unmistakable warmth of accent. Dr. Sandeep Marwah smiled and invited him to sit. The man appeared to also be suffering from a cold. Out of habit, Marwah ji asked:

"What will you have? Tea?"

The man replied: "Tea I am not drinking."

Marwah ji said pleasantly: "All right then — coffee?"

The man answered: "Coffee I have given up."

Marwah ji looked at me, then back at the visitor, and asked: "Shall I get you some water then?"

To which the man responded, with complete ease: "Water also I will not drink." There was a brief pause. Then, in a voice so low it was almost to himself, Dr. Sandeep Marwah murmured: "Toh zeher pi lo." — "Then have some poison." I caught every word. My composure collapsed entirely, and I could not hold back my laughter. Fortunately, the visitor did not hear it. Marwah ji instantly rearranged his face into an expression of complete seriousness, as though nothing whatsoever had occurred. After the visitor left, he permitted himself the smallest of smiles. That is his way — to say what needs saying, and yet leave no one uncomfortable. Even now, the memory of it brings a smile without warning.

What these incidents reveal is that Dr. Sandeep Marwah is not simply a man weighed down by serious responsibilities. He knows that approaching life with lightness is itself an art. His humour is never aimed at diminishing anyone — it is aimed at easing the moment. He uses laughter not as a weapon but as a salve: against stress, against fatigue, against the accumulated weight of a demanding life. Perhaps this is precisely why, despite so much pressure, so much activity, and so many responsibilities, he is able to remain balanced and centred. His humour is a kind of armour, quietly protecting him from the harshness that life can bring. This living, laughing side of him makes him all the more human — and it teaches something worth remembering: that even at the summit of success, one must not forget how to laugh. For the person who can truly laugh is the person who is truly living. This chapter is dedicated to that colour in his life — the colour of laughter, which shines on even amid all his serious achievements.

13

A Teacher Who Instructs as He Walks Through Life

There are certain people who give direction to life not only through their work but through their words — whose speech is not merely oratory but a distillation of experience, something that settles deep within the listener. Dr. Sandeep Marwah is one such person. To sit with him in conversation is not simply to discuss a subject; it is an opportunity to understand life itself. I say this from personal experience, for there have been many occasions when, wishing to share a new idea, a new plan, or a new perspective, he has turned to a small circle of people — and I have been fortunate enough to be among them.

One day I was seated with him in the middle of a discussion when a young man walked in. His face held reverence, his eyes held curiosity, and his manner was gentle. He appeared to be a student of the institution who had recently completed his course and had come to seek blessings — a scene that is common there, for people regard Dr. Sandeep Marwah not merely as the head of an institution but as a guide. What passed between them that day became a profound lesson not only for that young man but for me as well. With complete ease, Dr. Sandeep Marwah said to him: "Remember — in life, it is through work that success comes." The moment I heard it, I found myself saying, almost involuntarily, "What a thing to say." It may seem a simple sentence, but it holds within it one of life's deepest truths. He went on to explain to the young man the centrality of action in human life — that success does not arrive through some miracle, but is the accumulated result of good work done consistently. He told him that people often make success the goal while forgetting action altogether, when the truth is that if work is done in the right direction, with full heart and honesty, success follows of its own accord. He also said that good work must not be for oneself alone — it must extend to society and to others, for when a person adds selflessness to their efforts, their progress ceases to be personal and becomes something larger. The satisfaction on the young man's face was clear, but I was inwardly thinking that this lesson was not for one student — it was for all of us. At every stage of life, at every age, this principle of action remains equally relevant. That day I understood, with a new clarity, that Dr. Sandeep Marwah is not merely the administrator of institutions — he is a teacher of life, one who turns every occasion into a lesson.

Another incident comes to mind that reveals his reflective, almost poetic way of thinking. During a well-attended event, he was addressing the audience from the stage when he shared a small, seemingly ordinary experience — but one whose meaning ran deep. He described how, one day, he was sitting in his garden when an orange seller passed by on the road, calling out repeatedly: "Achhe meethe santre..." — "Sweet, fine oranges...” Most people would hear this as background noise and think nothing of it, but his ear caught something else entirely. He said: “In that voice, I heard ‘sang tare’.” And then he explained: if in life one finds the right company — sang — then life is carried across — tare — the difficult ocean of existence is crossed. This was not wordplay for its own sake — it was a living philosophy. He went on to say that a person’s life is made or broken by the company they keep, and that with the right companions, the right thinking, and the right guidance, even the hardest circumstances can be navigated. The audience sat in a kind of quiet wonder. To draw so profound a truth from the call of a fruit seller on the street — only a truly sensitive and contemplative mind can do that. In that moment, I felt it clearly: for Dr. Sandeep Marwah, the school of life is not somewhere separate from daily existence — it is daily existence itself. Every scene, every sound, every ordinary moment is a lesson waiting to be read.

His teaching moves with him wherever he goes. He does not instruct only in a formal classroom — he weaves learning into conversation, into examples, into the stories of his own experience. He does not merely talk with people; he engages them in dialogue so deep that it compels thought, that it quietly changes something within. This, perhaps, is the truest mark of a good teacher: one who does not merely give information but gives vision. By this measure, Dr. Sandeep Marwah is a teacher in the fullest sense. One of his most often-repeated observations — and one that is particularly relevant today — addresses the tendency among young people to avoid participation. Today’s students frequently shy away from activities in school and college, afraid of the stage, afraid of failure, held back by hesitation or simply by inertia. He has understood this tendency deeply, and I have heard him say from many a stage: "Bhaag lene se bhaagya badalta hai" — "Fortune changes through participation." As simple as the sentence is, it carries great force. He explains, time and again, that if you do not step forward into an opportunity, how can your circumstances change? Opportunities open only for those who reach out to meet them. The fear of losing, the dread of criticism, the anxiety of failure — these, he says, are all natural parts of life, but life cannot be lived by avoiding them. Until a person puts themselves forward and tests their own capability, they will never discover the possibilities that lie within them.

Dr. Sandeep Marwah's words are not motivational statements delivered for effect — they are practical principles for living. What makes them remarkable is that he never reaches for weighty philosophical language; he says something profound in the simplest of words, and this is precisely why his words travel directly to the heart. He inspires young people to dream, but he equally teaches them that the path to realising those dreams runs through effort, through good company, and through wholehearted participation. For me, every moment spent in his presence has been a lesson — sometimes hidden in advice given to a student, sometimes in the call of an orange seller, sometimes in a single sentence spoken from a stage. He reads life, understands it, and then shapes it into words and passes it on to others. This chapter is dedicated to that aspect of him: a man who builds institutions, but who builds people even more. Who is not merely a professional but a guide. Who does not merely speak but teaches. And who teaches that success comes through work, that life is carried by good company, and that fortune changes through participation.

14

The Magic of Poetry That Travels from Stage to Soul

Sandeep Marwah's personality is as vast as it is sensitive. Most people know him as a successful media educator, organiser, founder, and cultural ambassador — but those who have heard him on stage know that within him also lives a poet: one who does not merely decorate language but touches the soul. His love for poetry is extraordinary. I have personally heard him recite his well-loved verses across many platforms and on many different subjects, and each time it has felt not like a speech being delivered, but like a heart speaking directly to other hearts.

His conviction is that whenever one stands on a stage, one must weave poetry, proverbs, and small illustrative examples into one's address. He says that this transforms a speech from the merely informational to the genuinely inspiring — that it stirs not only thoughts but feelings. A bare fact, he observes, may reach the mind, but poetry descends straight into the heart. And it is only when the heart is moved that change becomes lasting.

The range of his poetry, when one looks at it closely, encompasses all of life — philosophy, the resolve of self-confidence, the inspiration to persist through struggle, and the tenderness of devotion — all present together. Consider these lines:

"From all directions,
Let the auspicious and the beautiful flow,
May thoughts and feelings of goodness,
Fill the heart each day,
Let this sacred earth become heaven
Through my own efforts, O merciful one."

Within these lines lies not merely a prayer but a resolution. He does not look to others to transform the world — he asks what his own efforts might do to make this earth into something closer to paradise. This orientation is precisely what sets him apart: he teaches his listeners that change begins from within, not from without.

Another poem carries his message of self-reliance and inner confidence:

"Let man be his own creator,
Awaken the faith that lives within you,
Walk not in footprints that are already fading —
Make your own path, of your own choosing.
Depend upon the light of your own soul,
And become your own sun."

When he reads these lines from the stage, the hall fills with applause, because these are not merely words — they are a direction for living. He urges young people to understand that walking in another's footsteps may be easier, but forging one's own road is true success. To depend upon one's inner light and become one's own sun — this message carries a particular urgency in today's age of fierce competition.

On the impermanence of what we cling to, his vision is equally searching:

"Leave the shade of the tree, O traveller,
Leave the shade of the tree.
Watch how the afternoon shifts and falls,
And the shadow itself changes form."

These lines carry the plain truth of life: attachment to comfort is the enemy of progress. The shelter that protects today may become tomorrow's illusion. To keep moving is life; to stop is not. In the same spirit, his verses on love and surrender flow with equal ease:

"I have become yours entirely —
Test me whenever you will.
Our eyes have already met;
Now let heart meet heart.
O flame, for your sake
I have become the moth.
Come and see for yourself —
I have lost my reason in you.
I have fallen prostrate before you —
Now, at least, lift me up.
I have become yours entirely —
Test me whenever you will."

When he reads these lines, an altogether different feeling fills the air — not merely devotion to a beloved, but the symbol of complete faith in one's purpose, one's work, one's God. He teaches that when love for one's goal takes hold, even struggle becomes a form of worship.

His poems also carry a message of determination:

"Those who are faint of heart never begin —
Fear holds the lesser person back.
Those of middling resolve abandon the road
When adversity crosses their path.
But the best among us endure every difficult way,
And advance with firm, unhurried steps,
Pushing every obstacle aside."

Many young people, on hearing these lines, recognise something of themselves. They come to understand that it is hardship that builds character. He says repeatedly that those who never begin out of fear forfeit life's opportunities altogether, and those who give up halfway return from the very threshold of their destination. But the finest are those who see every difficult path through to its end. Some of his lines are so delicate they touch the heart directly:

"Without melody, Saraswati comes not;
Without a teacher, knowledge is not found.
A swan without water finds the world thus —
As Bharat found God."

In these words, love of nation and of the spirit meet beautifully. He regards India not merely as land but as an article of faith. And in another verse, deeply philosophical:

"The road has its own allure, in its proper place —
But the will of those who walk it is also needed.

Though love may shed a hundred thousand tears,
The consent of the heavens is also needed."

This is one of life's truest observations. Effort alone is not enough — the cooperation of time and circumstance is equally necessary. He teaches that a person must keep working, but must leave the outcome to God or to nature.

The call to illuminate and to persist runs through many of his lines:

"Illuminate the sky and earth,
Keep giving light where darkness dwells.
With the force of a great wind,
Sweep away the darkness of despair."

And then there is his enduring counsel to smile through everything:

"Somewhere a full moon, somewhere no moon at all,
Somewhere thorns, somewhere a slippery path,
Somewhere desert, somewhere clouds —
But keep smiling as you walk,
And the very directions will grow bright."

These lines are the essence of his philosophy. Circumstances will keep changing — sometimes the silver of a full moon, sometimes the scorching of a desert, sometimes a stumble, sometimes a binding — but to keep walking with a smile is the truest form of courage.

One incident has stayed fresh in my memory. I was seated in his office one day, in the middle of a discussion, when a group of middle-aged visitors arrived together. They touched his feet in greeting — and then, remarkably, one of them began reciting his poems from memory. Gradually the others joined in, picking up the lines. They were all former students of his institution who had completed their courses years earlier. They said: "Sir, the poems you spoke — we still remember them to this day." In that moment I understood what the power of words truly is. Lines spoken from a stage years before were still alive inside these people. I thought to myself: surely these poems must have steadied them at some difficult turning point in their lives. Another occasion is equally worth recounting. I was at a prestigious fashion show in Delhi when a gentleman I did not know signalled me from across the room to come and sit beside him. When I did, he smiled and said: *"Your Marwah sahab is a remarkable man. I know several of his poems by heart."* I assumed he was being playful and said lightly, "Well, if you know them, let's hear them." And to my astonishment, he began. One after another, he recited Sandeep Marwah's verses from memory. I sat in silence. That day I understood: a person cannot be present everywhere, but their goodness, their words, and their influence arrive before them.

The particular quality of his poetry is that it carries no unnecessary complexity — it says something profound in the simplest language, and rather than burdening the listener, it fills them with energy. His verses do not exist to ornament the stage; they exist to light the lamp of the mind. For him, poetry in a speech is not decoration but a spiritual practice. He regards poetry not as literature alone but as an instrument of leadership, believing that a true leader is one who can awaken hope in people — and that the most powerful means of awakening hope is the sensitive word. This is why he reads poetry from every stage, offers examples at every occasion, and sends inspiration through every exchange.

When we look at Sandeep Marwah today — as a successful educator, organiser, cultural ambassador, and motivational speaker — we should also look for the poet within him. It is the poet who gives his personality its balance. It is the poet who keeps him sensitive. It is the poet who makes his words endure. Through poetry, he has kindled self-confidence in countless young people, drawn many out of despair, and dedicated still others more deeply to their goals. His poems did not remain confined to the stage — they became part of people's lives. And perhaps this is the truest mark of a real poet: when words leave the page and enter life itself, when lines become memories that walk alongside us, when a voice remains present even in its absence. His love of poetry is not a personal pastime but a mission — to awaken feeling, to give direction to thought, and to make life meaningful. There is in his words a genuine power: the power to become a lamp in darkness, and to give the tired traveller the courage to walk on.

15

The Discipline of Excellence and the Cleanliness of Character

Sandeep Marwah's personality is rich with many dimensions, but if one quality were to be singled out for special mention, it would be his love of cleanliness and his unwavering insistence on excellence. He is not merely a successful educator, media figure, or organiser — he is a person who lives life as a disciplined art. The more I have come to know him, the more clearly I have seen that this perfectionist nature runs through everything he does, every decision he takes, and every interaction he has.

His eye is extraordinarily sharp — and this sharpness extends not only to ideas but to the physical environment around him. Whether it is a stage, a classroom, the wide grounds of Marwah Studios, his own office, or a colleague's room, his gaze invariably finds something that an ordinary eye would pass over. Where others see everything in order, he immediately identifies that small lapse which, left unaddressed, could diminish the dignity of the space. I have personally seen him bend down in the grounds of Marwah Studios and pick up a scrap of paper, a piece of polythene, a stray tissue — carrying it to the nearest dustbin without a moment's hesitation and without any self-consciousness whatsoever. He does not do this for effect; it is simply part of his nature. For him, cleanliness is not an outward appearance but a state of mind. He believes that a person who cannot maintain order in their immediate surroundings cannot bring discipline to their thoughts and actions either. There have been many occasions when faculty, deans, and numerous staff members were all present and no one noticed anything amiss — yet the moment he arrived, his eye went directly to the point where improvement was needed. I have more than once been left quietly astonished by this alertness. It is not merely the act of inspection — it is the feeling of responsibility. For him, every corner of the institution is a reflection of his own integrity.

This habit of his becomes, in time, a lesson for everyone around him. I freely acknowledge that I have learned a great deal from him — the importance of cleanliness, the importance of presentation, and above all, the habit of not dismissing small things as unimportant. He often says that excellence does not arrive suddenly; it is the result of countless small corrections, accumulated over time.

Two incidents stand out as particularly illuminating of this aspect of his character. The first involved the Dean of our institution's mass communication department — a man of considerable academic talent, but one who paid little attention to his own appearance. I was seated in the Dean's office that day when Dr. Sandeep Marwah arrived. His habit, whenever he enters the Marwah Studios grounds, is never to go directly to his own office after stepping out of the car. He stops along the way to speak with students, staff, and faculty, and I have often seen him in conversation even as he climbs the stairs — a habit that reflects his human side as much as his discipline. That day, the moment he stepped into the Dean's cabin, his eye fell on something immediately: a crumpled coat hanging on the window latch. The Dean himself was wearing a loose, old-fashioned sweater, and the room was in a state of general disorder. The words came out of him at once — "What is this? Why has Saidulajab been recreated here?" I could not help laughing. Saidulajab is a famously chaotic neighbourhood in Delhi; his point was plain — this was not a disorganised back lane but an international institution. A dean's bearing is itself the face of the institution, and if his room and his appearance were in disarray, what message would that send? There was irony in what he said, but no cruelty — only the impulse to improve. The Dean understood immediately and composed both himself and his room without delay. That day I came to understand that true leadership is precisely this: the willingness to point out a failing, while never humiliating the person who holds it.

The second incident belongs to the world of journalism. During the Global Festival of Journalism, a journalist arrived at Marwah Studios dressed in a manner that was entirely without professional dignity — chappal on his feet, his appearance unkempt and careless. Most people would have let it pass, telling themselves that personal choice deserves respect. But Dr. Sandeep Marwah's view of these things is different. He believes in the wholeness of life, and his conviction is that a person who does not respect themselves cannot respect their profession. He took the journalist aside and said to him quietly: "Being a journalist does not mean being dishevelled. You are the author of your own image. If you do not keep yourself in order, how will society take you seriously? Present yourself well — this is not only your dignity, but the dignity of the entire media world." There was no reprimand in his words — there was direction. He does not correct people to bring them down; he does it to lift them up. This is his perfectionism in its truest form: reaching from outward cleanliness all the way to inner discipline.

His attentiveness does not stop at individuals. The decoration of the stage, the punctuality of a programme, the seating arrangements for guests, the quality of the microphone, the lighting — every detail, large and small, falls within his field of attention. A single small carelessness, he believes, can undermine the impression of an entire event, and so he leaves nothing to chance in preparation. His days are extraordinarily full, yet he never accepts disorder with the excuse that there was no time. For him, that is not an explanation — it is an evasion. He says that the proper use of time is a person's truest identity, and that a person who cannot keep their workspace in order will not be able to keep their thinking in order either. His love of cleanliness is not only physical but mental: he believes in clarity. Ambiguity in a decision is something he cannot accept. He wants every person to understand their responsibility with complete clarity and to carry it out with full dedication. This is why those who work with him gradually become disciplined themselves — not because they are told to, but because they watch him and understand.

He leads by example before he ever gives an instruction. When the founder of an institution bends to pick up a scrap of paper, the staff feel a quiet shame that they should have noticed first. When the chairman himself is punctual, no one else feels at liberty to arrive late. Many people mistake perfectionism for rigidity, but in his case, it is not rigidity — it is commitment. He holds himself to the same standard he expects of others, and this is precisely why his words carry weight. People understand that what he says, he has already lived.

In an era when carelessness and going through the motions are increasingly common, his disciplined and watchful nature is genuinely inspiring. He teaches that success does not come from talent alone — it comes from discipline and order as well. Your environment shapes your thinking, and your thinking shapes your future. His life is proof that when a person takes even the smallest details seriously, the larger goals become remarkably more attainable. His sharp eye is not there to find fault — it is there to find opportunity for improvement.

The time I have spent in his company has taught me that excellence is not a destination but a continuous process — that to strive each day, each moment, to be a little better is what true progress looks like. His love of cleanliness and his pursuit of perfection are not merely habits; they are a philosophy. He holds that until a person brings order to themselves, they cannot bring order to the world. And perhaps this is precisely why every institution he has built, every event he has organised, and every stage he has created carries within it a particular elegance and dignity that is unmistakably his own. His life teaches us that greatness begins in the humble moment when you bend down and pick up a piece of paper from the ground — for it is in that moment that the true meaning of responsibility and leadership begins.

16

The Journey from Tiny Drops to an Ocean

"Drop by drop a river forms, and river by river an ocean."

I have heard this saying from Sandeep Marwah's lips more times than I can count. The first time he said it, it struck me as a pleasant motivational phrase and nothing more. But as time passed and I came to know him more closely — listening to his struggles, watching the way he worked — I understood that this was not merely a saying for him but a philosophy of life. Every decision he has taken, every effort he has made, every difficulty he has faced seems to be a shadow cast by this very idea: the resolve to gather tiny drops, one by one, until a vast ocean stands where nothing stood before.

One day, sitting in the sprawling grounds of the Film City, he drifted into old memories. All around us was the hum of activity — modern buildings, studios at work, students moving to and fro. He said quietly: "No one wanted to come here once." I looked at him in surprise. He continued: "This entire land was sandy. The villagers from nearby would graze their cattle here. After dark, there was the fear of thieves and petty criminals. In that kind of place, even dreaming of building a film city seemed like madness to people." There was a particular light in his eyes as he spoke — the light that comes from remembering struggle. He went on: "When Marwah Studios was being built, this was the bank of the Yamuna. Dig even a little and water would come up. We would dig the foundation at night and return in the morning to find it full of water again. Drain it, start over. How many nights passed like that, I have lost count."

I watched the emotions move across his face — the memory of difficulty on one side, the quiet satisfaction of having overcome it on the other. He often says that there is no substitute for hard work, and his daily life was the living proof of that statement. Arriving at the studio earliest in the morning, remaining absorbed in work until late at night — as though time existed for him only as a means to reach his goals. He once laughed and mentioned his old car. "I had a Maruti 800. It had no air conditioning, because I couldn't afford the extra twenty-five thousand rupees for it." He smiled at the memory. "In the Delhi summers, making run after run between Delhi and Noida, my back would be soaked in sweat. I'd have to make the journey several times a day because a great deal of what the studio needed simply wasn't available in Noida then — the city itself was still being built."

As I listened, the picture formed before me: dusty roads, unfinished buildings, limited means, and a person bent on giving shape to a dream. He described how things shifted gradually — from the Maruti 800 to a steam-powered car, then to larger vehicles — but this change did not come suddenly. It was the result of years of labour, struggle, and patience. Yet life, as he has always known, is not made only of achievements. He spoke of one episode that represents the most difficult chapter in his story. Building the studio was consuming enormous resources, and the means available to him were stretched thin. He decided to try his hand at property dealing — made contact with some builders, invested his own money, and encouraged certain acquaintances to invest as well. His intentions were honest, his purpose clear: a little additional return would help fund the studio's construction. But fate did not cooperate. The builder proved unreliable and died unexpectedly. The project was left suspended. The money was trapped. His own funds were gone — and so was the money of those who had invested on his word. One by one, people began to come to him. "Sahab, we invested because you told us to."

Whenever he tells this part of the story, he pauses for a moment. Then he looks at me and asks: "Can you imagine how much I lost? If I told you the number, you'd faint right where you're sitting." There is a faint tremor of pain in his voice, but there is also steadiness — the steadiness of a man who has already found his way through. He said: "My intentions were honest. I made a mistake, but the responsibility was mine. I paid back every single person, one by one." I sat looking at him in silence. In an age when people reach for excuses to escape what they owe, here was a man who had himself suffered a devastating loss and yet resolved to restore every rupee to every person who had trusted him. This is not ordinary.

He then described how his father's guidance reached him during those difficult days. "When the liabilities had mounted," he said, "my father told me it was time to change the car." I asked in surprise: "When you're trying to pay off debts, why change the car?" He smiled. "That's exactly what I said. And my father replied — 'That's why I'm telling you to buy a

Mercedes. If you go around in an auto, people will lose faith in you. Their trust must be kept alive.'" I was silent for a moment. The depth of that thinking struck me: trust is built not only through words but through presence and bearing. He followed his father's counsel and bought the Mercedes. People were surprised — but their faith did not waver. Slowly, he worked his way out of that financial tangle, and the edifice built on the foundation of trust grew strong again.

Another quality emerges clearly from his telling: a deep reverence for family and an unshakeable belief in the blessing of parents. He often says, "I have reached where I am because of my parents' blessing" — and when he says it, there is no pride in his voice, only humility. In more intimate moments, he sometimes admits that his thinking has grown a little old-fashioned now, that there are occasional clashes of perspective with the younger generation, and that these moments of friction sometimes weigh on him. But in the very next breath, he shakes off the gravity with a smile and says, in his theatrical way: "That is why no one says anything to me!" — and the room fills with laughter. This is the quality that draws me to him most: the balance of seriousness and ease. On one side stands the disciplined, hardworking, goal-driven man; on the other, the storyteller who can lighten any atmosphere with a turn of humour. To move from narrating a struggle to cracking a joke in a single breath — it is as if he is saying that life is not a burden to be carried but a festival to be lived.

When I look at his life as a whole, it is clear that he built his ocean drop by drop. There was no miracle, no sudden magical success. Dreams were sown in sandy ground, waterlogged foundations were emptied and dried again and again, journeys were made with sweat-soaked backs, financial blows were absorbed, hard decisions were taken to preserve trust, and through all of it, patience was never surrendered. Today, when the Film City gleams in the light and the grandeur of modern studios catches the eye, very few people know how many countless drops went into its foundations — drops of effort, of sacrifice, of courage, and of faith.

Spending time with him has often left me with a clear sense that success does not come from resources alone — it comes from vision and patience. The person who can see possibility in sandy land, who can find a lesson in failure, who will not abandon honesty even in loss, and who keeps a smile alive even in disagreement — that is the person who can turn drops into an ocean. His story is not merely the achievement of one individual; it is the story of a way of thinking that says: no small effort is ever wasted. Every drop matters. Every day's labour, every difficult decision, every responsibility faithfully met — all of these, gathered together, take on a vast form in time. Now, whenever I hear him say "drop by drop, a river forms...", the saying has become a reminder for me as well: that no great dream is realised in a single day. It is the result of countless small steps, relentless effort, and unshakeable belief. The truth is that Sandeep Marwah's life is itself the living explanation of that saying. He did not merely build an ocean — he also taught us that in the process of building one, every single drop deserves to be honoured. And perhaps this is his greatest quality of all: to carry the memory of struggle within him and still keep smiling, and to see each new morning as the opportunity to add one more drop.

17

The Foundation Laid Beneath the Ocean

People often ask me: "How do such large events keep happening at your Marwah Studios? Every few days there is some national or international programme, a seminar, a conference, an awards function — how is all of this possible?" I smile and give the same answer every time: "Our Marwah sahab is very active. He is always doing something or other. And honestly, his doing teaches the rest of us a great deal as well."

Working with him has taught me one thing clearly: he never regards any event as merely an "event." For him, every programme is an opportunity — to bring people together, to advance ideas, and to lay a foundation that may, in the years to come, become the basis of some larger transformation. On one occasion, an important meeting of the Asia Pacific Union was organised at Marwah Studios. The organisation's president was J. S. Saluja, and Sandeep Marwah was its patron. It was a national-level event, distinguished guests were expected, and the assumption was that a healthy number of people would attend. Our team set to work. Under Sandeep Marwah's guidance, we are capable of designing a programme for our own studio in two hours — who is to be invited, how the stage is to be arranged, what the backdrop will be, in what order the speakers will address the audience — everything falls into place in an orderly manner. Years of experience and continuous practice have given us this ability. But when the organisers are from outside, we observe them deliberating for hours — perhaps because they organise one event a year while we manage several every week. The difference that experience makes reveals itself naturally.

The day before the meeting, Sandeep Marwah mentioned quite casually: "Getting an audience together has become very difficult these days. I can ask the students of my AAFT school — they'll help as volunteers and take care of the audience as well. Getting 150 people seems difficult to me." Some of the organisers looked slightly uncomfortable at this. Perhaps the thought occurred to them that if students were brought in, food would have to be arranged for them and the logistics would grow. They said, a little hesitantly: "Let's call just a few students." In the end, a limited number of students were invited. When the day of the event arrived, not even half the expected attendance materialised. The chairs at the back of the hall had to be removed to conceal the empty spaces. In that moment, I felt the weight of Sandeep Marwah's foresight. He had spoken from experience, not from guesswork.

This was a national conference, and former Union Minister Smt. Meenakshi Lekhi had been invited as the chief guest. The stage was set, the speakers were addressing the gathering in turn. When Sandeep Marwah's turn came, he spoke with characteristic ease and confidence about his connection with the Asian Union. He described how he had made the word "Asian" a part of his identity — that placing "Asian" in the names of institutions such as the Asian Academy of Film and Television was not merely a choice of words but a vision: the vision of threading the countries of Asia together through a single cultural strand. He also shared that ninety-two countries have chosen him as their cultural representative in India — a fact that left many in the room visibly surprised. He went on to say that he had been continuously offering scholarships to students coming from across Asia, so that borders would not become barriers on the road to education and culture.

As I listened, I was thinking to myself: these efforts may look modest from the outside, but what a vast vision lies behind them. In the office, such questions come up from time to time. Some say: "What will opening forums with ninety-two countries actually achieve?" Others ask: "What will giving scholarships change?" We run nine forums named after national heroes. One gentleman once went so far as to say: "What will organising a programme on Netaji Subhash Chandra Bose accomplish?" As many mouths, as many opinions. Everyone has their view. But one thing is clear: Sandeep Marwah is resolute in his course. What he has decided to do, he does. He listens to every perspective, but takes his decisions from his own experience and vision — and once a decision is made, the work is always seen through.

At the close of the programme, Meenakshi Lekhi addressed the gathering, speaking at length on the challenges and possibilities of the Asia Pacific region. Then, turning to the organisers, she said: "Whenever you hold events in the future, involve students as much as possible. If you want to connect the nations of Asia, the new generation must be brought along.

And with students present, the problem of audience will also not arise." Her words were a direct validation of what Sandeep Marwah had said from the very beginning. She continued: "It is good that discussions and conferences are held — but do people actually act on these ideas?" And then, praising Sandeep Marwah's scholarship initiative, she said: "This is an excellent effort. To unite Asia, words alone will not be enough — action is needed. And that is what Sandeep Marwah is doing." In that moment, I felt that sometimes time itself becomes a witness, validating a person's thinking. What had been met with quiet scepticism only a short while earlier was now being spoken of with appreciation from the stage.

I recount this episode here because it is not merely the story of one event. It is the story of a way of thinking that reaches beyond ordinary limits. Perhaps you and I cannot see that far ahead — we look at today's results, while he sees the possibilities of the years to come. He once said: "Keep laying foundations beneath the ocean. Keep working. And keep waiting until the day people begin to see the building above the water." At the time, this struck me as somewhat philosophical. Now I understand what he meant. A foundation laid beneath the ocean cannot be seen. People ask: what is the use? What are the results? What has been achieved? But the person who works on quietly, patiently, continuously, knows that one day that very foundation will become the base of something vast.

His small, steady steps — building forums, giving scholarships, organising cultural programmes, holding events in the names of national heroes — may not yield immediate results. But he is constructing a way of thinking. He is building a network within which countries can speak to each other, students can exchange with one another, and culture can serve as a bridge. Working with him has taught me that leadership is not the act of giving orders but the act of giving vision. He does not merely assign us tasks — he gives us a way of thinking. He says: "Think about what you are doing today in the context of five years from now. Only then will you understand its true worth."

When doubt arises, he smiles. When someone objects, he listens. But he does not allow himself to be diverted from his goal. Perhaps this is why Marwah Studios has become not merely a studio but a continuously active platform — a place where ideas are born, programmes are held, and a new generation is prepared. Today, when people ask why so many events, why so many forums, why so many initiatives, I remember that same phrase: "Keep laying foundations beneath the ocean." Every programme is a brick. Every scholarship is a stone. Every conversation is a layer of mortar. Gradually, invisibly, the foundation grows stronger. And one day, when people see the building that stands on foundations of trust, culture, and education, perhaps they will understand that none of it happened suddenly. It was the result of years of invisible labour.

This is his essential quality: he believes in the process before the result. He concentrates on the preparation before the applause. And perhaps this is why, wherever he stands, activity begins of its own accord. He has taught me that in order to realise large dreams, one must first accept invisible labour. Everyone wants to be seen on the stage — but very few are willing to lay foundations beneath the ocean. He is among that rare few: a person who believes not in noise but in structure; not in discussion but in action; and who knows with certainty that one day the building will be visible — the building whose foundation he has been quietly laying for years.

18

A Living Example of Creativity

Very few people truly understand that human beings are born not merely to survive, but to remain creative. God has given every person the capacity to create — some create with words, some with colours, some with music, some with ideas. Yet the irony is that most people never recognise this creative power within themselves. They become entangled in routine, confined within limits, and never attempt to awaken the creator that lives inside them.

I have come to know Sandeep Marwah with great closeness. Working with him, listening to him, understanding his decisions — through all of this I have experienced that he is not merely an administrator, an organiser, or a founder. He is, at his core, a creative person. His creativity is not confined to the stage; it shows itself in the way he works, in his conduct, in his conversations, and in his vision. He has the habit of seeing every task from a new angle — and it is precisely this habit that sets him apart from the ordinary.

Throughout the year, numerous events take place at

Marwah Studios, but four major festivals carry a special identity — among them the Global Fashion Week. An ordinary fashion week means designer clothes, models on a ramp, lights, music, and applause. But under Sandeep Marwah's leadership, this event becomes not merely a display of garments but a platform for cultural dialogue. I have often wondered what it is that he does differently — what it is that fills the same stage with an entirely new meaning. The answer lies in his thinking. We have forums of ninety-two countries: nations that have chosen Sandeep Marwah as their cultural representative. This is not a merely formal relationship — it is the construction of a cultural bridge. Connected to this, he put forward one day a simple but striking idea: "Since we represent these countries, why not give space on the Global Fashion Week ramp to their traditional costumes as well?" The moment one heard it, it seemed entirely natural — and yet the surprise was that no one had thought of it before. The idea was embraced and immediately set in motion. Models were dressed in the traditional attire of various countries, and the name and cultural identity of each nation began to emerge as part of the backdrop. But Sandeep Marwah did not stop there. On the day when a particular country's costumes were to be featured, he personally invited the ambassador of that nation. This was not a formal gesture — it was a symbol of respect and partnership. Simultaneously, he asked students to prepare a brief report on that country: to research its history, culture, food, and dress. The students worked with genuine enthusiasm, and when that country came alive on the ramp and was presented from the stage, the moment was no longer just a fashion show — it had become a cultural celebration. I have seen many ambassadors grow emotional in those moments. They did not come merely as spectators; they came filled with pride at seeing the soul of their country brought to life on that stage. Their eyes shone. They expressed their gratitude warmly, and in those moments I felt what creativity truly means: it means connecting people, touching feelings.

His characteristic quality is that he never leaves an idea incomplete. When he saw that ambassadors were attending the events, another thought was born: "Why not present the traditional food of that country as well?" And with that, a new chapter began. He assigned this responsibility to the AAFT School of Hospitality and Tourism. Students researched recipes, prepared dishes, and one by one the cuisines of different countries began to be displayed. The Global Fashion Week was no longer a presentation of garments alone — it had become a multidimensional cultural experience where the audience could see that country, hear about it, and taste it. I have personally savoured the food of countless countries at these gatherings. Every stall held a new story, every dish carried a culture within it. When ambassadors saw their country's food presented with such respect, their enthusiasm only grew — they spoke with students, encouraged them, and in this way a fashion show became a living stage for international relations. All of this became possible simply because someone chose to look at an ordinary event with an extraordinary eye.

A more recent example came during the Global Festival of Journalism, when a special fashion show was organised. One ramp walk on that occasion was dedicated to the BRICS Plus nations — Sandeep Marwah had recently been appointed as the Brand Ambassador for BRICS Plus countries, a significant achievement in itself, but one he refused to leave merely as a title. He immediately suggested to the school's head: "Why not dedicate a special ramp walk to the BRICS Plus nations?" The idea came, and action followed at once. As I sat at that fashion show watching the costumes of BRICS Plus countries appear on stage one by one, a feeling arose in me unbidden: what a pace of thought. He not only gives ideas — he gives them momentum. Many people remain confined to ideas: they discuss, they plan, but acting on them takes time. What distinguishes Sandeep Marwah is that the distance between his thinking and his doing is remarkably small. This is precisely what makes him effective.

His creativity is not confined to events alone — he inspires students to be creative as well. He tells them: "Don't copy, create. Don't walk on someone else's path, make your own." He wants every student who leaves to carry not just a degree but a new way of thinking. In the office, we sometimes discuss his new ideas amongst ourselves. Someone will say: "What will connecting so many countries actually achieve?" Another will ask: "Why are so many festivals necessary?" But with time we see that those small efforts take the form of a large network. An ambassador from one country meets a representative from another. Students become familiar with different cultures. New possibilities for dialogue come into being. I have come to feel that a creative person finds opportunity in every circumstance. Where an ordinary person sees an event, a creative person sees a platform. Where someone sees a fashion show, he sees a means of cultural diplomacy. Where someone sees a dish of food, he discovers the possibility of international conversation.

Working with him has also made me understand that creativity is not limited to the arts — it is a way of thinking, a capacity to see problems from a new angle, an art of building balance between tradition and the modern. When I look back today, I find that behind every event held at Marwah Studios, a creative thought is hidden. No programme is merely a programme — it is a message. No fashion show is merely fashion — it is a cultural bridge. No festival is merely a celebration — it sets the direction of the future. And all of this has been possible because one person chose not to keep his creativity to himself, but gave it the form of an institution, a movement, and a culture.

To be truthful, I am sometimes left in quiet astonishment at the speed of his thinking. An idea arrives, a decision is made, and within days it begins to appear on stage. This is not merely organisational ability — it is the result of creative energy. Perhaps this is why people keep asking: "How do so many events happen at your place?" And inwardly I think: because here, creativity is alive. Here, every day holds the effort to think and do something new. Here, creation is not a word — it is a way of life. Watching Sandeep Marwah, my conviction only deepens: human beings are indeed born to remain creative. The only difference is that some recognise their creativity, and some let it pass unnoticed. Those who have recognised it light the flame of creation not only in their own lives but in the lives of countless others. Sandeep Marwah is one of those people — a person who turns every stage into an opportunity for creation, every event into a means of dialogue, and every idea into reality by giving it the momentum it needs. It is precisely this creativity that makes him singular, and that continues to inspire us without end.

19

Trust Preserved in Documents

Among all the qualities I have come to know and understand in Sandeep Marwah, one stands apart most distinctly: the habit of systematically documenting every event, every programme, every meeting, and even the smallest activity. Many people organise events, hold programmes, meet others, pose for photographs, and move on. But very few are those who preserve each occurrence, record it, and make it part of history.

His belief is that memory cannot be relied upon. He often says with a smile: "I can't even remember what I ate yesterday — and we're talking about events and occasions." There is a deep meaning hidden in that remark. He understands that memories grow dim, people change, time passes — but a description recorded on paper becomes an authentic proof. That document, in time, becomes a witness to history. Today, under his International Chamber of Media and Entertainment Industry, forums have been established with ninety-two countries, each of which has chosen him as their cultural representative in India. This is not merely a formal title — it is a responsibility. Sandeep Marwah himself chairs all of these forums. But the most remarkable aspect of this entire system is his documentation practice. A separate file has been created for each country — not a nominal file, but a living document. From the day a country's forum was established, a chronological record of its activities has been maintained. If an artist from that country visited Marwah Studios, or a filmmaker, a writer, a poet, a cultural worker, or a media representative — the full details are recorded in that file: who came, when they came, for what purpose, what conversations took place, which programme they participated in — all of it preserved in orderly form.

I have witnessed many times that when the ambassador of a country visits our studios and Sandeep Marwah places before them the complete account of their country's forum activities, they are genuinely astonished. They are struck by the fact that every link in the cultural exchange between their country and this institution has been kept safe: which delegation came, which programme was held, which artist performed — everything present with documented evidence. This is not merely administrative efficiency — it is proof of seriousness. It makes clear that Sandeep Marwah does not regard his work as a formality but carries it out as a mission. For him, the connection with each country is a responsibility, and he honours it with complete sincerity.

The list of these ninety-two forums is itself like a map of the world — the Indo-Afghanistan Cultural Forum, Indo-Algeria Film and Cultural Forum, Indo-Argentina, Indo-Armenia, Indo-Azerbaijan, Indo-Bahamas, Indo-Belarus, Indo-Benin, Indo-Bosnia, Indo-Brazil, Indo-Bulgaria,

Indo-Cambodia, Indo-Chad, Indo-Chile, Indo-China, Indo-Comoros, Indo-Cuba, Indo-Cyprus, Indo-Czech, Indo-DPR Korea, Indo-Egypt, Indo-Equatorial Guinea, Indo-Ecuador, Indo-Ethiopia, Indo-Fiji, Indo-Gabon, Indo-Gambia, Indo-Georgia, Indo-Germany, Indo-Ghana, Indo-Guatemala, Indo-Guyana, Indo-Hungary, Indo-Iceland, Indo-Iran, Indo-Iraq, Indo-Ireland, Indo-Israel, Indo-Jamaica, Indo-Kazakhstan, Indo-Kyrgyzstan, Indo-Lebanon, Indo-Lesotho, Indo-Liberland, Indo-Lithuania, Indo-Malaysia, Indo-Maldives, Indo-Mauritius, Indo-Mongolia, Indo-Montenegro, Indo-Morocco, Indo-Myanmar, Indo-Namibia, Indo-Nepal, Indo-Nigeria Film Association, Indo-Oman, Indo-Palau, Indo-Palestine, Indo-Panama, Indo-Papua New Guinea, Indo-Paraguay, Indo-Peru, Indo-Philippines, Indo-Polish Film Association, Indo-Principality of Monte d'Agrela, Indo-Romania, Indo-Russia, Indo-Rwanda, Indo-Senegal, Indo-Serbia, Indo-Slovak, Indo-Slovenia, Indo-South Africa Film Association, Indo-South Korea, Indo-Spain, Indo-Sudan, Indo-Suriname, Indo-Tajikistan, Indo-Timor-Leste, Indo-Trinidad and Tobago, Indo-Tunisia, Indo-Turkey, Indo-Turkmenistan, Indo-UK, Indo-Uruguay, Indo-USA, Indo-Uzbekistan, Indo-Venezuela, Indo-Vietnam, and Indo-Wales Creative Forum.

This list is not merely a compilation of names — it is the expanse of a vision. Behind each forum lie countless meetings, conversations, programmes, film festivals, cultural evenings, scholarships, and stories of exchange. And the documentation of all of it does not allow these things to remain merely memories — it gives them a permanent identity. People sometimes wonder why such meticulous filing and record-keeping is necessary. But when a chronological account of ten years of cultural dialogue with a country is placed before its ambassador, the power of that documentation becomes unmistakable. It ceases to be paper — it becomes proof of trust.

I believe this quality is what sets Sandeep Marwah apart from many others. He does not merely do his work — he also creates the history of his work. He does not merely hold events — he preserves those events in documents, leaving behind an example for the generations that follow. In a time when so much glitters briefly on social media and disappears, a description recorded on paper gives permanence. It testifies that all of this was not mere publicity but a continuous effort — a committed journey. I have come to feel that documentation is not merely the process of keeping records — it is an expression of responsibility. It reveals how seriously a person takes their work. This habit of his is proof of his discipline, his foresight, and his professional commitment.

When he says, "What is written on paper becomes authentic proof," it is not merely a sentence — it is the essence of his way of working. He knows that when, in the future, someone asks what was done, when it was done, and how it was done, he will have not only the answer but the evidence as well. And perhaps this is precisely why his standing at the international level has continued to grow — because he is not merely a representative, but a responsible one. He does not merely add names; he honours relationships. And he preserves those relationships not in words, but in documents. Whenever I look at the files arranged in the cabinets of his office, they do not seem to me like ordinary paper. They seem like the story of countless meetings, smiles, conversations, and cultural bridges — all gathered together, with patience and commitment, by one person.

To speak plainly: Sandeep Marwah's success does not lie only in his events, his festivals, or the activities visible on international platforms. His real strength lies in the organised thinking that records every small step, preserves every effort, and authenticates every achievement. And I believe it is this quality that separates him from the crowd. He does not merely live in the present — he writes history for the future.

20

The Journalist Hidden Behind the Pen

Many people know Sandeep Marwah as a successful educator, founder, cultural ambassador, organiser, and visionary. He often says from various platforms that his journalism school — the AAFT School of Journalism and Mass Communication — is among the ten best schools of its kind in the world. Behind this claim lie solid arguments, lived experience, and real achievements; the standards he has set over the years in media education speak for themselves. But that is not what I wish to discuss here. I wish to speak of the person who sits not in front of the stage but behind it, putting pen to paper — the journalist hidden within Sandeep Marwah.

Over several decades of continuous engagement with print media, radio, and television, he came to know the media world from close quarters. He watched journalists at work, understood editors' priorities, and felt the process by which news is selected. From this long experience, he arrived at an important conclusion: that leaving aside a few senior and experienced journalists, most reporters often write in haste.

The pressure of time, the weight of competition, and the race to be first sometimes mean that accuracy is not given sufficient attention — statistics remain incomplete, names are misspelt, the full context of a speaker's remarks does not emerge, and the balance of language breaks down. These things affected him deeply. He understood the power of words. For him, a news report was not merely information — it was a responsibility. This is perhaps why, in the early days, he began writing press releases himself. He wanted whatever information went out to be precise, balanced, and presented in dignified language. There were times when newspapers did not give adequate prominence to his media activities — stories were shortened, sometimes not published at all, or the context was altered. This could have discouraged anyone. But his temperament is different: he knows how to convert disappointment into energy.

It was out of these very experiences that he took a bold decision — to establish his own news agency. And so Asian News Agency was born. This was not merely an institutional initiative but an idea: the idea of presenting news with the dignity it deserves. He has claimed that through this agency he has personally written and published more than five thousand news reports. Heard for the first time, the number may seem like an ordinary statistic — but when one looks at it more closely, its true significance becomes apparent. Writing a news story is not merely a matter of typing a few lines. It requires a complete understanding of the event, the accurate compilation of facts, the precise recording of names and designations of those present, an exact account of who said what, the purpose of the programme and its context — all of this must be kept in mind. And when this work is being carried out by someone who is himself the head of a large organisation, who carries hundreds of responsibilities, who remains occupied throughout the day in meetings, programmes, and administrative decisions — the task becomes all the more demanding. I have personally seen him sitting late into the night to prepare reports. After a full day of activity, when most people are settling in for rest, he sits before his laptop and shapes the day's events into words. On many mornings he rises early to complete stories left unfinished the night before. Despite being the head of the organisation, he has never let this practice lapse. This is not merely discipline — it is his dedication to journalism.

This continuous writing has another effect as well. When a person writes the news themselves, events, names, dates, and contexts stay naturally in their memory. This is why he often surprises the audiences in his halls. Without consulting any paper, he can introduce a guest in full — their position, their country, their institution, and even the context of a previous meeting. This is not only an exceptional memory — it is the result of sustained writing and alert observation.

Every year, the Grand Festival of Journalism is held at Marwah Studios, attended by senior journalists from across the country and abroad. From this very platform, distinguished honours such as the Mahatma Gandhi National Award for Journalism and the Global Excellence Award in Journalism are presented. Sandeep Marwah personally confers these awards upon senior journalists. When he stands on the stage and speaks of the dignity of journalism, of integrity and social responsibility, the resonance of experience is audible in his words. He is speaking not merely as an organiser but as an active journalist in his own right. Sitting in the hall on such occasions, I sometimes think: this is a person who has himself written thousands of news reports, who has understood the inner workings of media, who has brought journalism education to a position of global respect — what award would one give to him? Is there any recognition reserved for his own pen? Or is his greatest honour simply this — that he remains continuously active, continuously learning, and continuously writing?

The journalist within Sandeep Marwah is not limited to writing news alone. He also questions, analyses, and suggests direction. He does not teach his students only the technical aspects of reporting — he also tells them that the fundamental purpose of journalism is to make society aware. He says that when writing a story, a journalist must remember that their words have the power to shape how society thinks, and that words must therefore be chosen with care. His habit of documenting every event himself is also, in a sense, a form of historical writing. What seems small today may become part of a larger context tomorrow. The stories he has written could become material for future researchers. Seen in this light, his writing is not merely daily reporting but a long-term act of archiving.

Through Asian News Agency, he has also demonstrated how essential self-reliance is. If the mainstream media does not give your work its full due, it does not mean that your work is without value — you can build your own platform. This perspective has become all the more relevant in the digital age, where every institution and individual can develop their own means of communication. His writing also sets an example at a time when information floods every channel, the threat of fake news is real, and credibility has become a challenge. An educator who remains an active journalist himself is not giving his students only theoretical knowledge — he is offering them a practical ideal. What he teaches, he practises. What he practises, he also writes down.

Sandeep Marwah has been honoured more than fifteen hundred times on prestigious platforms across the country and around the world — but perhaps the honour of being recognised purely as a journalist still awaits him. Sitting in the hall, watching him present awards to senior journalists, a question rises quietly in my mind: will there come a day when a stage somewhere honours Sandeep Marwah for his uninterrupted writing, for his commitment to journalism, and for the standards he has set? Perhaps there will be such a day; perhaps there will not. But the truth is that through his own work, he is already creating that honour for himself. May his pen keep moving, may his words continue to give direction to society, and may the journalist within him remain ever awake — for when an educator himself becomes a journalist and writes, a remarkable meeting of education and journalism takes place. And it is in that meeting that the foundations of a strong journalism for the future are quietly laid.

21

A Courtyard of Faith, Energy, and Sanctity

I have often heard people say that whenever they enter the premises of Marwah Studios, they experience a particular kind of positive energy. Some call it good vibrations, some call it peace, some call it inspiration. But whatever name one gives it, there is always within that experience a feeling of sanctity. Sandeep Marwah himself describes Marwah Studios as a sacred place. For him, it is not merely an institution, a studio, or an educational campus — it is the holy temple of media in northern India, from where the lives of hundreds of thousands of young people have been shaped. Over the years, many great figures from across the country and the world have walked through these grounds — from film, journalism, literature, politics, culture, and spirituality — sharing their thoughts and leaving behind the mark of their presence and their blessing. He often says that any person who has ever come to this campus — whether as a student, as a guest, or simply to take a class — is someone at whose feet we bow with reverence. These are not merely words; they are a feeling. And it is this feeling that has made the place all the more sacred.

I have felt this sanctity myself. Working here, I have had experiences that awakened within me a particular reverence for this place. I serve here as Director of Broadcasting, and there came a time when I needed to get the Grant of Permission Agreement signed by the Ministry of Information and Broadcasting for the radio operations. The task sounds simple enough in the telling, but in practice it was far from simple — paperwork, departmental formalities, round after round of follow-up. There were moments when it felt as though the process would never end. But with patience and perseverance, it was finally accomplished. The joy of that moment was difficult to put into words. I immediately sent a WhatsApp message to Sandeep Marwah informing him that the agreement had been signed. His reply came at once — three short letters: "JMD." I could not understand at first what it meant. The next day, when I came to the office, I asked Vinay ji — who was the General Manager of Marwah Studios at that time — what "JMD" meant. He smiled and told me: "Jai Mata Di."

In that moment, I understood that the foundation of Sandeep Marwah's success is not only hard work and managerial skill — it is also deep faith. When I later learned more about his family background, this devotion became even clearer. His parents used to visit Vaishno Devi every year. On his maternal side as well, there was a strong atmosphere of devotion to the Goddess; his maternal uncle was a particularly ardent devotee. These impressions, it seems, settled into his consciousness from the very earliest years of childhood.

The atmosphere I have witnessed at Marwah Studios during the Navratri days is something extraordinary. Throughout all nine days, a special spiritual energy pervades the campus.

Prayers are offered at the temple, and prasad is distributed. I have personally received prasad many times from the pandit — barfi, banana, apple, orange, arranged in a small plate. That offering is not merely sweets or fruit — it is a symbol of blessing. When the flame of the lamp is lit, it feels not like an ordinary light but like the unbroken flame of faith, illuminating the entire campus.

Upon entering Marwah Studios, one is immediately greeted by a magnificent temple of Lord Shiva. The figure of Shiva, established in a vast and serene posture, calms the mind at once. In the midst of a day's rushing, meetings, and programmes, whenever one passes before that temple, the hands join in reverence of their own accord. There is one more particular detail I noticed at the temple: within it, a photograph of Sandeep Marwah's father has also been placed. This image says a great deal. On one side, devotion to God; on the other, reverence for one's parents — the meeting of both makes that place all the more consecrated. I have many times seen him pause before the temple on his way in or out and stand with joined hands. This gesture never looked formal — there was no performance in it, no ceremony. Only a simple, natural act of bowing. Perhaps this is what true faith looks like: not a display, but something connected to the heart.

He runs an organisation called the World Peace Development Foundation, through which numerous significant spiritual and social programmes have been organised at Marwah Studios. Respected religious figures, Shankaracharyas, sages and saints, and representatives of various traditions and schools of thought have all come here and shared their wisdom. I have myself sat through many such gatherings and listened to their discourses. These are not merely religious events — they are platforms for dialogue: conversations about peace, harmony, and humanity. Seeing all of this makes one thing clear: for Sandeep Marwah, faith is not only a matter of personal belief — it is also a means of social harmony. He is devoted to his own faith, and at the same time respectful of others'. This balance is what makes him singular.

His faith does not stay within the temple — it shows itself in his conduct as well. I have seen him help many people: sometimes contributing quietly to a student's fees, sometimes guiding a staff member through a personal difficulty, sometimes making a special arrangement for a guest — always without noise, always without fanfare. On many occasions I have heard him give courage to someone in despair. There is belief in his words and truth in his manner. He says a great deal through his actions. Rather than delivering grand speeches from the stage, he offers examples through what he does. When a person who has reached the summit of success remains humble, they become an inspiration for others — and this is precisely what Sandeep Marwah is.

I often wonder: does the sanctity of a place come only from the temple established within it, or from the intentions and feeling of the people who work there? In the case of Marwah Studios, I believe it is both. Here there is a place of God, but there is also the primacy of work. Here there is worship, but there is also labour. Here there is faith, but there is also discipline. When hundreds of thousands of students have their futures shaped here, when they train here to realise their dreams, when they leave and make a name for themselves across the country and the world — the place ceases to be merely an institution and becomes something more: a ground of quiet endeavour, a place where something is tested and refined.

Perhaps this is why every person who comes here experiences a different kind of energy.

For me, this place is not merely a workplace. It is a courtyard where I have witnessed both administrative struggle and spiritual equilibrium; where I have seen professional success alongside human sensitivity; where I have seen the ancient flame of faith burning amid modern media equipment. When people say that Marwah Studios has good vibrations, I am not surprised — because I have lived those vibrations. I have experienced them in the Navratri aarti, in the quietness of the temple, in the smiles of students, and in the humble namaskaar of Sandeep Marwah himself.

His spirit is pure. And when a person's spirit is pure, the place they build becomes pure as well. Perhaps this is why Marwah Studios is not merely a collection of bricks and mortar, but a living, energy-filled, and faith-soaked courtyard — where work and devotion walk side by side, and where every person who arrives leaves carrying something positive within them.

22

An Unplanned Journey and an Unforgettable Honour

There are times when Sandeep Marwah's ways are beyond anticipation. Without any prior notice, he appears at the door of my cabin, knocks, and says with a smile: "Come, let's go somewhere... we'll be back in an hour." In that moment, I am rarely mentally prepared. The day's meetings, files, and plans are all running through my mind. But saying no to him never feels right to me. Going with him almost always opens the door to some new experience.

That day was no different. I got up quickly and settled into the car with him. We drove out of Noida towards Delhi. Along the way he said very little — only that there was a good programme to attend. Before long we arrived at Vivek Vihar, Shahdara. There stands a grand hotel — the Leela Ambience. Large cars lined the entrance, and at the registration desk inside there was considerable activity. The atmosphere suggested a significant corporate event. When we entered the hall, I was taken aback. Nearly a thousand people filled the room — officers and employees from various companies, holding senior positions, all formally dressed, serious, and energised. As far as I could understand, the event had been organised by an agency whose purpose was to motivate employees. Some of the country's foremost motivational speakers and achievers had been invited to share their experiences and infuse fresh energy into the audience.

The moment Sandeep Marwah arrived, he was taken directly to the stage. The organisers welcomed him warmly — a shawl was draped over his shoulders, a memento was presented, and without delay the microphone was placed in his hands. I found a place on a sofa in the front row — a seat I chose deliberately, thinking I might be able to take some photographs if the opportunity arose. But I must confess: within a few minutes I had forgotten entirely about the camera.

He began his address, as he always does, with a poem. There was depth in his voice and confidence in every word:

Let man be his own creator,
Awaken the faith that lives within you,
Walk not in footprints that are already fading —
Make your own path, of your own choosing.
Depend upon the light of your own soul,
And become your own sun.

The hall rang with applause. It was not merely a poem — it was a declaration: a declaration of faith in oneself, of self-reliance. I watched as the people seated before him, who had until that moment been sitting in formal composure, straightened up in their seats. Some put their phones down; others opened their notebooks.

What followed, in my eyes, was historic. It was as if Saraswati herself had taken her seat upon his tongue that day. He began the story of his struggles: the days in Mumbai, the hours of waiting, the disappointment of films that were never released, the decision to return to Delhi, the dream of a film city in Noida, the criticism of people, the financial pressure, and then the founding of a new institution. He was not reading from a book — he was opening the pages of his own life. There was no artifice in his voice. It came directly from the heart. When experiences tempered by pain, difficulty, and struggle take the form of words, they carry a power that is entirely their own. He wove small, ordinary incidents together in such a way that each became a large lesson for living. A proverb here, a phrase there, a couplet woven in — each adding colour to what he was saying.

The hall of a thousand people had fallen completely silent. Only one voice was sounding — the voice of a man speaking from the deepest part of himself. Sitting in front of him, I could feel that his words were not reaching only ears but travelling directly to hearts. People were nodding, some with a brightness in their eyes, some with an expression of quiet gravity. He said that success does not come suddenly — it emerges from the furnace of struggle, refined by heat. He described how people walk away when things become difficult, how dreams are made the subject of ridicule, and how one begins to doubt one's own decisions. But if the flame of faith continues to burn within, the path forms of itself. He also spoke about the value of time — that the person who understands time has won half the world, and that those who do not honour time are not honoured by it in return. His words carried the truth of experience. These were not lines learned from books — they were lessons drawn from the heat of a life lived.

I glanced at my watch. He had been speaking continuously, without any paper, without any notes — only experience, only self-possession. A full forty-five minutes had passed, and I felt as though time itself had stood still. In those forty-five minutes, there was nothing left unsaid. Every dimension, every feeling, every struggle seemed to have found its way into words. I wished I had recorded the entire speech that day. But perhaps some things are not meant to be recorded — they are meant to be felt. That address was not merely the experience of listening; it was the experience of living.

When he stepped down from the stage, the scene changed entirely. The crowd surrounded him. Everyone wanted a photograph. Someone shook his hand, someone offered thanks, someone said: "Sir, what you said has changed the way I think." For half an hour he remained caught in that crowd. The next session was about to begin, but no one's attention was elsewhere. It was as if the energy of the hall was still held in the resonance of his words — as though the crowd were saying, silently: we have heard what we came to hear. We need nothing more. This is the greatest honour that can be given to any speaker — when the audience is connected from the heart.

That day, I understood something with great clarity. This man is not inspiring by accident. He has been refined by sorrow, difficulty, and hardship — as gold is purified in fire, his personality has been burnished in the furnace of struggle. Perhaps this is why there is such resonance in his voice, such truth in his words.

On the drive back, he was entirely at ease. No particular elation, no self-satisfaction — as if nothing especial had occurred. He said only this: "One should meet people, share one's experiences with them." For him, it was one more programme. For me, it became an unforgettable chapter.

Even today, when I recall that day, I hear the applause of the hall, the lines of the poem, and his reverberating voice. That was not merely a motivational speech — it was the essence of a life. And that day I understood what a true speaker is: not one who occupies a stage, but one who finds a place within hearts.

23

Respect for Women Above All

To truly understand any person's character, it is essential to observe how they think about society and how faithfully they bring those thoughts into practice. Many people speak of lofty ideals, but the reality is that living by those ideals is rarely easy. There are certain personalities, however, who do not remain confined to thought alone — who present their values to the world in a powerful and tangible form, through institutions, platforms, and action. Sandeep Marwah belongs to that category.

Throughout his life, he has not focused solely on personal achievement. He has consistently worked to create opportunities and platforms for different sections of society — which is why he has, over the years, established numerous forums and stages through which social, cultural, and educational activities can be advanced. The purpose of these platforms was never merely to organise events, but to give those people an opportunity who so often find themselves without a stage on which to display their talent.

Among these platforms, one of the most significant is the International Women Film Forum — not merely an organisation, but a powerful means of honouring women's talent, their hard work, and their contribution. His belief is that women occupy a position of extraordinary importance in society, and that if they are given the right opportunities and encouragement, they are capable of achieving remarkable success in any field. Through this forum, programmes are organised periodically that work to bring women's advancement, self-confidence, and contribution into the light — inviting women working across various fields, appreciating their achievements, and inspiring them to go further.

Beyond this, in order to honour women who are active in the workforce, he established an international award: the Sarojini Naidu International Award for Working Women. This recognition is given to women who, in the face of difficult circumstances, have continued to work and carved out an identity for themselves in society. The award takes its name from India's great poet, freedom fighter, and symbol of women's empowerment — Sarojini Naidu. This choice of name is itself a symbolic statement, for Sarojini Naidu represents a tradition in which women are not confined to the home, but play a significant and active role in the making of society and nation. To date, Sandeep Marwah has honoured several hundred women through this award. In his view, a woman who remains active in her professional field over a long period of time has already achieved something considerable — because a working woman must attend not only to her professional life, but equally to her family and social responsibilities. He often says that when a woman works for many years, she is not merely advancing her career — she is also confronting numerous societal assumptions, maintaining balance between her duties at home and outside, and that very balance is the proof of her patience, her strength, and her self-belief.

I have heard him speak from many stages on this subject, and whenever he speaks of respect for women, what one hears in his words is not formality but genuine feeling. He often draws on examples from his own life, making it clear that this is not a theme for speeches — it is part of who he is. In a world where many speak extensively of women's empowerment while a gap between word and deed remains, no such gap is visible in Sandeep Marwah. What he says, he lives. The Asian Education Group itself is a clear demonstration of this thinking: a safe and respectful working environment has been created there for women, they are given equal opportunity, and their talent is actively encouraged. In numbers, approximately fifty percent of those working with the Asian Education Group are women — not merely a statistic, but a reflection of the faith he holds in women's ability and commitment.

Whenever Sandeep Marwah speaks of his own journey, he makes special mention of three women: his mother, Smt. Sheila Marwah; his wife, Smt. Reena Marwah; and his elder sister, Smt. Poonam. He says that each of these three women has played a profoundly important role in giving direction to his life. When he speaks of his mother, the respect in his voice is unmistakable. He says that from her he received his traditional Indian values — that the qualities of family, discipline, hard work, and humility came to him from the atmosphere of his home. A mother's values are the foundation of any person's life; they are what give shape to character and point the way in difficult times. When he speaks of his elder sister Poonam, he often becomes visibly moved. He describes how there came a time when the family faced difficult decisions about whether his education could continue, and how his sister made the decision that her younger brother's studies must not be interrupted — even if it meant giving up her own further education. This was not merely a personal sacrifice; it was an expression of love and faith in her brother's future. Such sacrifices leave deep marks in the history of any family, and perhaps this is precisely why he speaks of his sister with such profound respect and gratitude.

When he speaks of his wife, Reena Marwah, a particular tenderness enters his voice. He recalls the years of struggle — the long hours of work, the nights he remained absorbed in his responsibilities until very late. He describes how she would wait for him for hours so that they could eat dinner together. This was not a small or isolated thing; it was a demonstration of the patience and understanding that stands quietly behind every successful person, year after year. No one's success belongs to themselves alone — it belongs equally to those who stand beside them in silence.

On one occasion, I had the opportunity to attend a wedding in the Marwah family, held at Delhi's renowned five-star hotel, the Maurya. The atmosphere was full of festivity and joy. On that occasion, Sandeep Marwah introduced me to his elder sister Poonam ji. I was meeting her for the first time, though I had already heard a great deal about her. I found her exactly as he had always described her from the stage — calm, gentle, cultured, and full of warmth. I told her that Sandeep ji often speaks of her from public platforms, and that it was wonderful to finally meet her. The wedding was noisy, and perhaps she did not quite catch my words. Sandeep Marwah gestured to her and said: "They are saying something to you."

This time she listened carefully. When I repeated myself — that he mentions her often on stage and that meeting her brought me real happiness — her eyes filled with emotion. Love and pride were both visible in them at once. She immediately began offering her blessings to Sandeep Marwah. Watching that moment, I felt with great clarity that any person's success is never only the story of individual effort — it is the story of an entire family's feelings, sacrifice, and belief.

Today, women's empowerment is widely discussed. Speeches are delivered and plans are formulated on many platforms. But real empowerment becomes visible when a person actually understands and honours the contribution of women in their own life. Everything I have observed in Sandeep Marwah — in his words and in his conduct — has made me feel that it was the manner in which his mother, his sister, and his wife stood by him through his journey that gave birth, within him, to a deep and genuine respect for women. I have always seen him treat women with great consideration. Whenever a woman comes to meet him, he does not merely perform a formality — he listens to her attentively, encourages her spirit, and inspires her to do something new. Perhaps this is precisely why the forums and institutions he has established show the active participation of women in considerable numbers. Because respect does not come from words alone — it is revealed through conduct. And when respect is genuine, it gives others the strength to move forward. In Sandeep Marwah's journey, this respect for women is not merely an idea — it is a living tradition, one that began in his family and has now, through his work, reached out to touch society at large.

24

A Mind That Listens to the Heartbeat of Time

Some people move through life carelessly, while others live it with complete alertness — for whom every day, every moment, and every date carries its own significance. They do not merely watch time pass; they understand it, cherish it, and make it meaningful through their actions. Sandeep Marwah is one of those people for whom time is never just a sequence of dates on a calendar. For him, each day arrives carrying a new possibility and a new opportunity within it.

Spend even a short while in his company and you will quickly understand how aware and sensitive he is to time. He always knows why today is significant and what is coming in the days ahead. This awareness is not merely a habit of remembering — it is an essential part of his personality. The kind of planning, discipline, and foresight required to run a large educational institution shows itself naturally in his temperament. His most remarkable quality in this regard is his capacity to plan. He prepares well in advance for upcoming events, special occasions, and important dates. Nothing happens by accident — behind every programme there is a thought, a purpose, and a preparation. There have been many mornings when I have arrived at the office absorbed in my routine work, unaware that anything particular was taking place, only to notice from the atmosphere or the preparations around me that something special was underway — that today was the founding anniversary of Marwah Studios, or of the Asian Academy of Film and Television, or a significant day connected to the International Chamber of Media and Entertainment Industry. And it always surprises me how seriously and respectfully he holds these dates in memory. For him, they are not formalities. He marks these occasions in such a way that those connected with them feel themselves to be part of something larger.

What is equally notable is that his awareness is not limited to the anniversaries of his own institutions. He remembers the national days of countries from across the world with the same reverence. This is particularly remarkable given that he has served as the cultural ambassador of, or chaired forums connected to, more than ninety countries. The associations themselves are considerable — but more significant still is the fact that he remembers and honours these national days through his platforms, extending this courtesy even to countries with which he has no direct formal relationship. For him, these are not occasions for perfunctory messages — they are symbols of respect and friendship.

In today's rapidly digitalising world, social media has become an important part of every life, and people share their thoughts, feelings, and experiences through it constantly. But on social media one also frequently encounters posts without apparent purpose or meaning — things put up without much thought. When I observe Sandeep Marwah on social media, however, I see an entirely different approach. He uses these platforms with great deliberation. I have never seen him post anything without purpose. Behind every post there is some idea, some message, or some achievement. He shares the activities, programmes, and accomplishments of his institutions. His posts make clear how seriously he takes his work and how equally essential he considers sharing it with the world. Occasionally he also posts about his family — and in these too there is a simplicity and warmth, as though he is not merely conveying information but sharing some beautiful moment of his life with friends and acquaintances. I say without any hesitation that it was from him that I learned the right way to use social media — that it can be a highly effective medium for reaching people with one's work, but only if used with responsibility and thought.

What is most striking is that he does this entirely himself. In today's world, prominent individuals and large institutions routinely engage agencies to manage their social media — writing content, designing posts, uploading them. Sandeep Marwah's case is entirely different. He designs his own posts, writes his own content, and uploads everything himself. Many people are surprised that a person as occupied as he is can find time for all of this — but perhaps this is precisely his distinction: he manages time so well that there is always room for what matters. On WhatsApp as well, his activity is considerable. He has created numerous groups connecting people from his institutions, colleagues, friends, and professionals from various fields, through which he keeps everyone informed of every achievement, programme, and new initiative. The effect of this is visible in an interesting way: when I meet different people, they often say to me, "We keep receiving posts from Sandeep Marwah ji." Many say they have never met him personally, but through his posts they feel connected to him.

People often ask me: "Who manages Sandeep Marwah's PR? It must be a big agency — what a large contract that must be." When I hear this, a smile comes to me naturally. I think to myself that if I told them the truth, they might not believe it — because the truth is that none of this is the work of any agency. It is the result of one person's dedication, discipline, and continuity. He manages the greater part of his own public communication himself, functioning in a sense as a one-man army: running his institutions, planning programmes, staying in conversation with people, and simultaneously reaching his work out to the world — all with a natural ease that leaves observers wondering.

None of this happens by magic. Behind it lies one simple but profoundly important habit: alertness. Alertness to how precious time is. Alertness to the fact that every day offers an opportunity to do something new. Alertness to the fact that if you want your work to reach the world, you must make a continuous and conscious effort to put it there. This is perhaps why, in Sandeep Marwah's life, every day, every hour, and every date holds a special meaning. He does not only live in the present — he begins preparing for tomorrow today. And it is this alertness, this discipline, and this continuity that transforms an ordinary person into an extraordinary one.

25

Steadfast in Duty and Discipline

There is an old saying that laziness is the root of ruin. This is not merely a proverb — it is a deep truth of life, one we witness unfolding around us every day. Many people keep deferring their work: today's task to tomorrow, and tomorrow's task to some uncertain future. Gradually this habit becomes a part of their character, and that same laziness becomes the greatest obstacle on the road to their growth. In my professional life, I have seen countless people who, despite being talented, fall behind simply because they do not value time.

But when I speak of Sandeep Marwah, his personality appears to stand in complete contrast to this tendency. I have never seen so much as a trace of laziness in him. It would be no exaggeration to say that he does not merely keep pace with time — he makes time keep pace with him. Every day, every moment of his life is filled with purpose, and he works with full energy and dedication to fulfil that purpose.

He is frequently travelling, both within the country and abroad. Often he participates in programmes in different countries in quick succession, attending meetings and discharging various responsibilities. Most people, after such schedules, cite fatigue — particularly using jet lag as a reason to distance themselves from work for several days. I have heard many people say they are unable to work for two or three days on account of jet lag. But with Sandeep Marwah, this never happens. For him, it is simply an excuse — not a reality.

No matter which corner of the world he returns from, the moment his flight lands at any airport in India, his next step is already decided. His programmes are fixed in advance, and he moves towards his next responsibility without any delay. On many occasions I have seen him go directly from the airport to a conference, meeting, or event. It is a remarkable example of his discipline and commitment.

This quality is precisely what sets him apart from the crowd. He does not consider how tired he is, or how long his journey has been. What matters most to him is his duty and his commitment. This is why he becomes an inspiration for anyone who wishes to achieve something significant in life.

One particular experience is worth recounting here, as it gave me the opportunity to understand his personality even more deeply. An awards show was to be organised, named "Perseverance," to be held at the Radisson Blu Hotel in Dwarka, Delhi. It was a grand event with several distinguished figures from across the country and abroad in attendance, including ambassadors from various countries. Sandeep Marwah had been invited as the chief guest and was also to be honoured at the function. I had been entrusted with the responsibility of anchoring the entire programme.

At the time, Sandeep Marwah was occupied at his university — AAFT University of Media and Arts — in Raipur.

I remained in continuous contact with him, keeping him informed of the programme's status. As is often observed with many events held in Delhi, they are announced on a grand scale but the preparation behind them is not always equally organised.

On the day of the event, when his flight landed in Delhi, he immediately called me and asked about the situation. I told him that most guests had arrived and some were on their way. Without any hesitation, he said he would come directly to the venue. This did not surprise me at all — it is simply his nature. He arrived on time. As soon as he reached, I told the organisers we could begin. But the organisers asked me to wait a little. When I asked why, the answer that came back shocked me deeply: the awards had not yet arrived.

The situation was acutely uncomfortable. On one side, a large-scale event, distinguished guests, Sandeep Marwah present as the chief guest — and on the other, an oversight of this magnitude. I was at a complete loss about what to do. To manage the situation and buy some time, I thought we could at least complete the lamp-lighting ceremony. But even by then the awards had not arrived. Left with no choice, I began anchoring so that the programme could at least keep moving. Sandeep Marwah sat in front of me, gesturing to ask when the programme would actually begin. I tried to convey the situation to him through gestures as well.

Time kept passing and the programme somehow continued to limp forward. The awards finally arrived only when the event had reached its final stages. People were then honoured as best as was possible in the circumstances. In several cases, only a single award was used for photographs, with other recipients assured that their recognition would reach them later.

The entire experience was a lesson for me. That day I understood why people hold the programmes organised at Marwah Studios in such high regard. There, everything happens on time, in an orderly and professional manner — because behind it all is the thinking and discipline of Sandeep Marwah. The following day, when I spoke with him about it, he approached the entire experience with remarkable calm and positivity. He said that this country still has a great deal of room for improvement. He himself had been exhausted, yet he had arrived on time and fulfilled his responsibility. When I said that attending that event had been a waste of time, he smiled and said: "No — we learned what one must never do when organising a programme."

This perspective of his is genuinely inspiring. Where most people in such circumstances would only complain, he tries to extract a learning from every experience. For him, every situation is an opportunity — to understand something new and apply it to his work.

Sandeep Marwah's life teaches us that success does not come merely from dreaming big — it requires discipline, punctuality, and sustained effort to bring those dreams to life. It is only by setting aside laziness and making the most of every moment that we can make our lives truly meaningful. He is not merely a person — he is an idea: the idea that if there is genuine dedication and commitment within us, no obstacle can prevent us from moving forward. His life is a living demonstration that it is the person who respects time who can truly make time work in their favour.

26

His Food and the Plate of Belief

In any person's life, their habits and their beliefs play a deeply significant role. These habits are not merely part of a daily routine — they are a reflection of personality, of values, and of thought. Some people adjust their principles to suit circumstances, while others remain steadfast in their convictions. Sandeep Marwah's life belongs to the second kind — where even a habit that appears ordinary reveals the depth of his character.

Sandeep Marwah is a strict vegetarian. From childhood to this day, he has never once touched non-vegetarian food. Simple as this sounds in the telling, it is quite remarkable — particularly when one understands the family environment in which he grew up. During a casual conversation in the office one day, I had the opportunity to spend some time with him, and the subject of food came up. He shared an interesting detail from his childhood. He told me that his parents were extremely sensitive about his vegetarianism. When he was young, non-vegetarian food was occasionally prepared at home — this is quite common in Punjabi families. But on those days, he would simply not eat the home-cooked meal. He would quietly go to a nearby dhaba and bring back roti, dal, and sabzi, and eat that instead. His parents observed all of this. They knew how firm their son was in this regard. No doubt they tried to reason with him more than once, but he never compromised on this conviction — not even once.

This is particularly noteworthy because the family atmosphere in which he was raised was one where non-vegetarian food was not unusual at all. In Punjabi households it is frequently part of the regular diet. And yet, Sandeep Marwah never accepted it as part of his own life. It had become not merely a matter of food preference but a part of his personal belief and the principles by which he lived.

I had the opportunity on one or two occasions to accompany him on foreign trips, and these journeys gave me a closer view of this aspect of his nature. On one occasion, we travelled with a media delegation to Tashkent, the capital of Uzbekistan. In our honour, a grand dinner had been arranged at a traditional Uzbek restaurant — a truly lavish spread. The table was laid with a wide variety of dishes, most of them non-vegetarian. At that time I did not know him as well as I do now, and my eye kept travelling towards him. I wanted to see what he would do in such a setting. Kebabs, grilled meats, soups, and various local preparations covered the table, and the other media representatives were enjoying them with great enthusiasm. But I watched Sandeep Marwah quietly and naturally select only the vegetarian options, eating with complete ease and composure — only what was consistent with his principles. And crucially, he never once behaved in a way that suggested he was different from others or that he was in any way uncomfortable. He sat at the same table, participated in the same conversation, and remained entirely part of the same occasion. I have never seen him eat separately or make anyone feel that he was setting himself apart from those who eat non-vegetarian food. For him, it was a personal choice — not an occasion to comment on anyone else's.

This balance is itself a remarkable thing: to remain steadfast in one's own principles while at the same time fully respecting the choices of others. A similar occasion comes to mind from a media delegation visit to Baku, the capital of Azerbaijan. There too a fine dinner had been arranged in our honour. The organisers, knowing that guests had come from India, had made a special effort to include some Indian dishes — among them stuffed parathas, thinking this would particularly please the Indian visitors. We were all seated at the table, eating and conversing, when Sandeep Marwah picked up a small piece of a stuffed paratha and placed it in his mouth. My eyes fell on him at that exact moment. His wife, Reena Marwah, who was travelling with us, immediately said quietly that the paratha might have a non-vegetarian filling. Without the slightest hesitation, he removed the piece from his mouth and set it aside. There was no awkwardness on his face, no irritation. It was a small moment, but it told me a great deal about his character — that he was so alert to his own principles that even an inadvertent lapse was corrected at once.

At Marwah Studios as well, where programmes and events are held regularly with guests from across the country and the world, the food arrangements are consistently vegetarian. Everyone who works there knows that most events are catered entirely with vegetarian food. This too is an extension of his personal beliefs — though it does not mean he fails to respect the preferences of others. One occasion stands out clearly in my memory. The Ambassador of Ghana was present at one of the programmes, and after the event, when the meal was arranged, he appeared somewhat uncomfortable to find that no non-vegetarian food was available. It was perhaps an unusual experience for him. Sandeep Marwah understood this with great sensitivity. He felt that honouring a guest was as important as remaining true to his own principles. And so, at the next event, he made special arrangements to ensure that non-vegetarian food was also available for the Ghanaian representatives. This decision speaks to the balanced thinking that is central to his personality: on one side, he does not compromise his own values; on the other, he ensures that his guests feel respected and at ease.

This balance is not easy to maintain — particularly for someone who travels to countries across the world, meets people from vastly different cultures, and encounters different kinds of food and traditions at every turn. Yet Sandeep Marwah has maintained it with remarkable ease throughout his life. He is fully devoted to his own beliefs, and at the same time he holds the beliefs and habits of others in equal respect. For me, this aspect of his personality has always been a source of inspiration. Because having principles is important in life, but it is equally important to live those principles with humility and with respect for others. His life teaches that when a person has true fidelity to their own convictions, no circumstance is capable of shaking them loose. And perhaps this is why, like so many other facets of his personality, this seemingly simple quality too makes him extraordinary. The food on his plate is never merely food — it is a symbol of his beliefs, his values, and the simplicity of his life. And when a person's life connects this naturally with their principles, they become an inspiration for others as well.

27

A Creative Personality Steeped in National Spirit

"Wherever we walk with joy and abandon,
Let sky and earth bow in that direction,
Citizens of a free homeland are we,
Every song of ours is like the clouds.
We take pride in our many provinces,
Each cherishing its own tongue —
And yet, above all else,
We are Indian, world, we are Indian."

These lines are not merely a poem — they are the outpouring of a feeling that rises from the heart and travels directly to other hearts. I have heard Sandeep Marwah recite these lines from many stages, with full enthusiasm and passion. When he reads them, it feels not as though words are being spoken, but as though an energy, a spiritual feeling, is spreading through the entire hall. The confidence, the love of country, and the sincerity in his voice compel every listener to break into applause. In that moment, the atmosphere transforms — an ordinary programme suddenly becomes a national celebration.

The most essential aspect of Sandeep Marwah's personality is that he does not merely speak — he translates every thought into action. His love for the nation is not confined to speeches; it is reflected in his work, in his thinking, and in every decision he makes. Whether it is filmmaking, education, or social activities — in every sphere, his underlying purpose is always to advance the country and society.

Whenever the conversation turns to patriotic films, or to subjects involving the nation, society, or the role of young people, he is always at the forefront — not only promoting these themes but giving them new direction. Whether it is the National Cadet Corps, Scout and Guide activities, or any initiative aimed at instilling discipline and patriotism in the younger generation, he supports them from every platform and inspires young people to understand their responsibility towards their country.

As a filmmaker too, he has produced several films that bring forward stories of patriotism and sacrifice. In particular, his films on the martyrs of the Kargil War are not merely a means of entertainment — they are a tribute to those brave sons of the soil who gave their lives in defence of the country. Through these films, he has not only kept the stories of the martyrs alive, but also made a sincere effort to help the new generation understand that the freedom we enjoy today has behind it the story of countless sacrifices.

One particular occasion comes to mind when Sandeep Marwah introduced me to an organisation called Metamorphosis, which was engaged in making films about martyrs. Although his own production house, Marwah Film and Video Production, was also continuously working in this direction, through this organisation too he gave broader shape to this mission of patriotism. As part of this endeavour, a film was made — Ek Major Ki Virasat (A Major's Legacy). It was a documentary based on the martyrdom of Major Dwivedi, presenting the story of his sacrifice in the Kargil War in a deeply sensitive and powerful manner. I had the honour of directing this film, and it remains one of the most emotionally profound and proudest experiences of my life.

The film's screening was held at an auditorium near Dhaula Kuan in Delhi. The scene of that day remains fresh before my eyes. There was a particular gravity and reverence in the hall. When Sandeep Marwah arrived, the respect he received was not only for his work but for his personality and his contribution. That day, one thought kept returning to me: a man who works across so many diverse fields, who makes his presence felt everywhere despite an incredibly demanding schedule — how does he manage to be of service to every section of society? How does even his small drop, added to this vast ocean, create such a large ripple?

When I met Major Dwivedi's family, the moment was deeply moving. As his wife shared her experiences, both pride and pain were audible in her voice. There were tears in her eyes, but those tears carried a strange luminescence — the luminescence of pride in her husband's sacrifice. Both their daughters were present as well, and watching them see their father's story unfold on screen was a scene that shook something deep within the heart. That day I understood that films are not merely stories — they are a medium for emotion. And this opportunity came to me only because of Sandeep Marwah. He not only trusted me but gave me a platform through which I could express my own feelings for the country through my work.

Sandeep Marwah is not confined to film and media alone.

He is also associated with several important institutions of the Government of India — including the Ministry of Skill Development and Entrepreneurship, the Bureau of Indian Standards, and the NSDC. Through these organisations, he plays an active role in the country's development, ensuring that young people receive the right direction and opportunity.

His greatest quality is that he does not merely carry the spirit of patriotism within himself — he connects the people around him to that same spirit as well. Among his students and faculty members, he is always trying to awaken a sense of national identity. For this purpose, he has established several forums through which he periodically connects people to different ideologies and great personalities: the Jawaharlal Nehru Forum, Mahatma Gandhi Forum, Netaji Subhash Chandra Bose Forum, Pandit Deendayal Upadhyaya Forum, Sardar Vallabhbhai Patel Forum, Shaheed Bhagat Singh Forum, Ram Manohar Lohia Forum, Swami Vivekananda Forum, and Ganesh Shankar Vidyarthi Forum. These are not merely names — they are a chain of ideas that connect young people to the great leaders of the country and to their thinking.

I have witnessed many times how students take an oath at convocation ceremonies. That oath is not merely a formality — it is a promise: to fulfil one's responsibility towards one's institution, one's society, and one's country. When hundreds of students take that oath together, the scene is deeply inspiring. I have also heard Sandeep Marwah call out "Bharat Mata ki Jai" and lead others in it many times. This is not merely a slogan — it is a feeling that deepens the love and respect for the country within every heart.

If one were to attempt to capture Sandeep Marwah's entire personality in a single sentence, it would perhaps not be wrong to say that he is a person whose creativity and patriotism are complementary to each other. Wherever he goes, he leaves behind not only the impact of his work but also a thought, an inspiration, and a new energy in the hearts of people.

In today's world, when people are increasingly absorbed in their personal interests, personalities like Sandeep Marwah remind us that true success lies not in what we do for ourselves, but in what we do for society and the nation. His story teaches us that if the intentions are noble and the thinking is broad, even one person can bring about change in an entire society. Hidden within every initiative, every idea, and every action of his is a single message — the nation first. And perhaps this is precisely why he has become not merely a successful person, but an inspiration.

28

One Person, Countless New Initiatives

Sandeep Marwah is a person of extraordinary talent. He undertakes creative work continuously and with originality — and crucially, he does not simply do it and forget it. He maintains a complete and careful account of everything he has accomplished. He has carried out numerous initiatives that can legitimately be counted among the first of their kind in the country.

1. Noida Film City

If we speak of Noida Film City, it was the first film city in northern India and the second in the country — brought into existence on 28 March 1988 through the efforts of Sandeep Marwah. The country was fortunate to see this in the last seventy-five years. From the sixteen studios of the Film City, three hundred and fifty channels broadcast news round the clock in three shifts to one hundred and sixty-two countries. Approximately twenty thousand media professionals work here, and because of this, the livelihoods of one hundred and fifty thousand people are sustained.

2. Marwah Studios

Similarly, Marwah Studios, established on 10 March 1991 as northern India's first professional film studio — is also a credit that belongs to Dr. Sandeep Marwah. In northern India at that time, there was no environment of any kind around film and media. The establishment of northern India's first film studio gave birth to many of the country's most respected television channels, including Zee TV, NDTV, Sahara Samay, Eenadu, ETV, Mahua, and Pragya. One can say that over the past thirty-three years, Marwah Studios has produced approximately four thousand five hundred television programmes for fifty channels, one hundred and twenty feature films in eight languages, and approximately five thousand training films.

3. Asian Academy of Film and Television

In the field of media, the country's first private film institution was launched on 22 July 1993 under the name Asian Academy of Film and Television. It became the first such institution in northern India and the third major film institution in the country. The Asian Academy gained recognition not only within India but internationally, attracting students from approximately one hundred and forty-five countries. Today, students trained at AAFT are making their mark across the country and the world, and the institution has grown into a large family of nearly thirty thousand students.

4. Film and Television Research Centre

The country's first Film and Television Research Centre (IFTRC) in the private sector is also the result of Sandeep Marwah's efforts, established in 1996. Through regular debates, discussions, workshops, and seminars on diverse subjects held under the IFTRC, media professionals from across the country and the world are connected to this centre.

5. Film and Television Club

To further strengthen the study of cinema, Dr. Sandeep Marwah established the country's first Film and Television Club, which provides a platform for filmmakers to screen their work at film festivals. Under the AAFT Festival of Short Digital Films, approximately three thousand five hundred films from around one hundred countries, made by three thousand directors, have been screened to date. Screenings, workshops, seminars, symposiums, and interaction programmes are organised regularly, and this tradition has continued uninterrupted for the past thirty-two years. Thirty-two years ago, the idea of such a film and television club was beyond the imagination of most people. The greatest contribution of this club has been the sustained connection it has created at the international level — something that may have existed nationally, but was happening internationally for the first time.

6. Radio Noida

Noida's first community radio station was also launched through Dr. Sandeep Marwah's efforts. Radio Noida was started seventeen years ago. Radio Noida 107.4 FM became known not only as the voice of Noida, but was also designated a "Lead Radio Station" by the Ministry of Information and Broadcasting. Over seventeen years of continuous broadcasting of socially committed programmes, this radio station has established its own distinct identity and place.

7. International Public Broadcasting Forum

The country's first International Public Broadcasting Forum (IPBF) was created with people interested in media and film in mind, with the objective of educating and raising awareness among them. The subjects and issues of the programmes broadcast through it are social in nature. The IPBF's purpose is to give new entrants in film and media the opportunity to make their first film — regardless of which film institution or field they come from. The reason behind starting it is itself quite moving. Sandeep Marwah recounts that a young man who had completed a course at a film institution was unable to make his first film for several years, and ultimately took his own life. When he read this news in the newspaper, he resolved that no one would lose their life for this reason again. He began inviting aspiring filmmakers to come and make films using his resources. To this day, he regrets that if only that young man had come to him, he would have allocated a film to him on the spot — the film would have been made at his expense and the tragedy could have been prevented. For this purpose, he provides infrastructure, equipment, and manpower — in short, a complete opportunity to make a short film.

8. International Women Film Forum

There are many women's forums, but there was no women's film forum at the international level. The International Women Film Forum was created with the purpose of bringing forward the talent of women associated with film, television, media, art, culture, and other creative arts — to nurture and develop them and provide a platform for them to come forward. Many programmes have been organised for women under this forum, and they have been continuously encouraged to advance. Under this initiative, the Dr. Sarojini Naidu International Award for Working Women was also launched, through which Sandeep Marwah has been honouring a hundred distinguished working women from India and abroad every year.

9. MSTV — Country's First Community Television

The country's first community television, MSTV, was also started through Sandeep Marwah's unique efforts. Under it, interviews have been conducted with distinguished artists, educators, businesspeople, scientists, media professionals, and people from various other fields, both from India and abroad. Very recently, it has been transformed into the country's first educational OTT channel.

10. International Children Film Forum

The International Children Film Forum (ICFF) is the country's first forum in the private sector dedicated to creative films for children, under which film training, film production, and an International Children Film Festival are organised. In addition, ICFF regularly hosts debates, screenings, workshops, seminars, symposiums, and interaction programmes. It also undertakes a careful study of films before organising a film festival for children.

11. International Chamber of Media and Entertainment Industry

The International Chamber of Media and Entertainment Industry is the world's first chamber to have been started by an educational setup. There may be ten thousand chambers across the world, but this is the only one entirely dedicated to the media and entertainment industry.

12. International Festival of Cellphone Cinema

The world's first Cellphone cinema festival was also launched by Sandeep Marwah, named the International Festival of Selfphone Cinema. According to him, nineteen years ago he started this festival in which half the inaugural film was shot in New York, USA, and the other half in India — both shot on mobile phones. In those days, films shot on mobile phones had little to offer in terms of quality, content, or editing. But today we live in an age of rapidly changing technology, where mobile phones are used in mainstream cinema productions. To have conceived of such an idea nineteen years ago was the work of someone truly extraordinary. This is why he has been honoured with the title of Father of Cellphone Cinema.

Sandeep Marwah always walks ahead of his own thinking, and it is for this reason that, in many ways, he has become the first to initiate things, both in the country and in the world.

29

A Cultural History Written in World Records

Sandeep Marwah is among that rare breed of personalities whose life is not merely the story of personal success, but a continuous journey dedicated to art, culture, media, and society. Through his actions, he has demonstrated that when vision is broad, thinking is global, and purpose is directed not inward but outward toward society, a person writes history through their own deeds. Today, Sandeep Marwah's name is spoken not only as that of a successful media professional, but as a visionary who gave India a new identity on the world map in the fields of film, television, and media — and who has established ten international world records.

Among his greatest achievements is the establishment of Noida Film City — the fastest-developing film city in the world, a conception that was far ahead of its time. Spread across a hundred acres, with seventy-five acres of outdoor facilities and twenty-five acres of vast indoor structures, the Film City is today a living centre of media production. Sixteen state-of-the-art studios function here continuously, and from this single location more than three hundred and fifty television channels broadcast around the clock to a hundred and sixty-two countries. These are not merely numbers — they are symbols of India's creative strength and its global acceptance.

The most widespread and human impact of the Film City is visible in employment. Approximately seventeen thousand media professionals work here in three shifts of eight hours each, every day. Beyond them, roughly one hundred and fifty thousand people earn their livelihoods indirectly through activities connected to the Film City. This is not only an industrial achievement — it is a powerful example of social and economic empowerment. It was in recognition of this extraordinary contribution that Sandeep Marwah received honours such as "Three Chairs," which reflect the many dimensions of his leadership and influence.

As the founder of Marwah Studios — northern India's first professional film studio — his name is written in gold. Over the past thirty years, more than four thousand five hundred programmes have been produced at this studio for over fifty television channels. He has been directly or indirectly associated with one hundred and twenty-five feature films in eight languages and approximately five thousand training films. Marwah Studios has been not merely a production centre but a laboratory of creativity — a place from which most of India's channels have received new thinking, new talent, and new direction.

Another historic achievement is the establishment of the Asian Academy of Film and Television — India's first private film school, located in Noida, of which he has been the president for the past thirty years. During this period, he has educated and trained more than twenty thousand media professionals from all twenty-eight states and six union territories of India, as well as from one hundred and forty-five countries worldwide. He designed seventy-five different courses at the certificate, diploma, and degree level, ranging in duration from three months to four years — a body of work in educational design that was accorded the status of a world record, testifying to his farsightedness in the field of education.

In the field of film production, he established yet another unique world record: becoming the producer of the greatest number of short films in the world, having produced more than three thousand three hundred films across virtually every possible cinematic genre. This is not simply a record of productivity — it is a story of opportunity created for others. He gave more than fifteen thousand amateur and professional filmmakers from over one hundred and twenty countries a platform to make and present their films. This work establishes him not merely as a producer but as a global mentor and inspirer.

His contribution to international festivals is equally unparalleled. He has given the country ten major international festivals: the Global Film Festival, Global Festival of Journalism, Global Literary Festival, Global Fashion Week, International Festival of Selfphone Cinema, AAFT Festival of Short Digital Films, ASMS Festival of Short Films, Children Film Festival, Country-Wise Festival, and Sufi Festival. All are of international stature, providing a shared platform for artists, writers, journalists, and filmmakers from across the world. Among these, the AAFT Festival occupies a particularly distinguished place, having completed its one hundred and fifteenth edition and thereby created a unique world record — offering more than three thousand directors the opportunity to present their films to international audiences. It has become not merely a festival but a powerful medium for global creative dialogue.

Sandeep Marwah has been actively involved in more than seven thousand events, remarkable not only for their number but for the diversity of their subjects — workshops, seminars, symposiums, dialogue programmes, festivals, book and music launches, dance and music performances, press conferences, national and international summits, foreign delegation visits, celebrity visits, painting and sculpture exhibitions, photography and textile exhibitions, jewellery exhibitions, fashion shows, beauty competitions, and much more. This level of activity establishes him as a true cultural catalyst.

He is the only person in the world to have presided over more than one hundred organisations spanning film, television, media, art, culture, and social work. In addition, the governments of ninety countries have appointed him as their cultural ambassador in India — a responsibility ordinarily accorded to heads of state, prime ministers, governors, ministers, ambassadors, or high commissioners, but conferred upon Sandeep Marwah on account of his cultural credibility and global influence.

Thirty-two years ago, he introduced the term "Film and Television Tourism" to the English lexicon. Perhaps very few understood its significance at the time, but today nearly every country is working with this concept. It is through this thinking that he has succeeded in attracting over three million visitors to Noida Film City — an achievement that is itself a landmark in the history of Indian tourism and media.

His coverage of the nineteenth Commonwealth Games Queen's Baton Relay is another unique world record. From Wagah Border to Jawaharlal Nehru Stadium, New Delhi —

spanning twenty-eight states, five union territories, a journey of twenty thousand kilometres, coverage of three hundred events in nine hundred cities, ten thousand photographs, and one thousand hours of film — all of this resulted in a new world record. One hundred and two radio programmes and one hundred and two short films prepared for global broadcast in one hundred and two days were also part of this achievement. The opening film of the Commonwealth Games was produced by Marwah Studios, and seventy-five AAFT students assisted foreign media during the Games. Sandeep Marwah himself was among the nine hundred athletes selected to carry the baton from Jaipur to Delhi.

Dr. Sandeep Marwah, associated with Noida, India, also established a unique global record when four books written about his life and work were launched within just twelve days, at four prestigious international venues in four different countries. This remarkable literary journey began on 1 September 2025 in Noida, where the first book was launched at Marwah Studios on the occasion of the inauguration of AAFT's one hundred and twenty-fifth batch. On 5 September, the second book was unveiled at a special ceremony in the House of Lords in the British Parliament, London. On 6 September, the third was released in Dublin, Ireland, at the sixteenth Indian Film Festival of Ireland. The fourth and final launch took place on 12 September at Ajyal Hall, Children's City, Dubai, during a celebration marking fifty years of cultural relations between India and the United Arab Emirates. This unprecedented literary achievement reflects Dr. Sandeep Marwah's global influence and contribution across the fields of media, culture, and education.

As for honours, Sandeep Marwah has been recognised

more than fifteen hundred times in India and abroad. Doctoral degrees from various universities, recognition at the House of Lords and the House of Commons in London, acknowledgement at the Welsh Parliament in Cardiff and the Bavarian Parliament in Munich, the Dadasaheb Phalke Foundation Award, the Gateway of Freedom from Poland, the Alexander the Great Award from Greece — each of these honours reflects his standing in the world.

And yet, despite all these extraordinary achievements, it is his humility that makes him greater still. He attributes all his successes and world records to his revered parents and to each and every person who has worked at the institution. For him, this journey is not over. It is only a beginning. In the years ahead, the world may well become witness to even greater achievements. Sandeep Marwah's life is proof that when dreams are large and resolve is unshakeable, a person becomes, in themselves, a walking world record.

rahi publication
A Publishing House
NEW DELHI

9 789391 532437

Printed at Repro India Ltd.